A HOUSE DIVIDED AGAINST ITSELF

ROBERT B. WINN

Gotham Books

30 N Gould St.
Ste. 20820, Sheridan, WY 82801
https://gothambooksinc.com/

Phone: 1 (307) 464-7800

© 2023 *Robert Winn*. All rights reserved.

No part of this book may be reproduced, stored in a retrieval system, or transmitted by any means without the written permission of the author.

Published by Gotham Books (September 2, 2023)

ISBN: 979-8-88775-475-8 (P)
ISBN: 979-8-88775-476-5 (E)

Because of the dynamic nature of the Internet, any web addresses or links contained in this book may have changed since publication and may no longer be valid.

The views expressed in this work are solely those of the author and do not necessarily reflect the views of the publisher, and the publisher hereby disclaims any responsibility for them.

PREFACE

A house divided against itself cannot stand.

Abraham Lincoln

And if a house be divided against itself, that house cannot stand.

Mark 3:25

FOREWORD

Two men met at Weehawken, New Jersey, on July 11, 1804. Both were prominent political party leaders of their time. They had come together to resolve a political dispute. After their meeting, the political careers of both were essentially over. Alexander Hamilton, the former Secretary of the Treasury of the United States and founder of America's first political party, the Federalist Party, was mortally wounded and only lived part of another day. The man who shot him, Aaron Burr, the Vice-President of the United States, was wanted in two states for murder. Burr had been elevated to the position of Vice-President because of his expertise in party organization.

Of the two men, Aaron Burr was more like the party politicians of today. He and Hamilton were just unfortunate to live in a time when party politicians were settling political disputes with dueling pistols instead of with microphones. Politicians of today would try to spread their contention to their political followers and let them fight it out.

Content

CHAPTER ONE 1

CHAPTER TWO 3

CHAPTER THREE 5

 CHAPTER FOUR 7

CHAPTER FIVE 14

CHAPTER SIX 18

CHAPTER SEVEN 23

CHAPTER EIGHT 29

CHAPTER NINE 34

CHAPTER TEN 39

CHAPTER ELEVEN 42

CHAPTER TWELVE 44

CHAPTER THIRTEEN 49

 CHAPTER FOURTEEN 56

CHAPTER FIFTEEN 62

CHAPTER SIXTEEN 67

CHAPTER SEVENTEEN 71

CHAPTER EIGHTEEN 75

CHAPTER ONE

In 1642 Charles I, King of England, declared war against his own Parliament. Charles did not see himself as an unreasonable king, but Parliament had taxed his patience. In the ensuing bloody civil war, the armies of the king were defeated by the armies of Parliament under Oliver Cromwell. The king was captured, sentenced to death for treason, and executed by beheading.

Parliament abolished the office of king forever, and England was declared to be a commonwealth and free state. Oliver Cromwell served as head of state with the title of Lord Protector of England until his death.

The death of Cromwell left Parliament with a problem they had not prepared to resolve. After an unsuccessful attempt to elevate Cromwell's son to the position of Lord Protector and some years of political confusion, Parliament requested that Charles, the son of Charles I, return to England from the European continent, where he had been living in exile, and become king. Charles graciously consented.

Charles II was not a good king. He had acquired some bad habits during his exile on the European continent. He was indolent, self-indulgent, and immoral. He did not have some of the good qualities of his father, Charles I, devotion to duty, courage, religious faith, and devotion to family and friends. But Charles II had observed his father's miscalculation. A king could be deposed and executed.

Consequently, Charles II was more adapted to getting along with Parliament than his father had been. Still, there were some things that a king needed to impose. While a disagreement that included war might be understandable to a king, regicide was not. The regicides had to receive the just punishment for their crime. So the thirteen regicides who had sat on the High Court and voted for the execution of Charles I were hanged and drawn and quartered. The bodies of the great Lord Protector Cromwell and some of his subordinates were dug up, hung in shrouds, and then buried in a common pit.

Parliament could understand how Charles felt. The Parliament that had warred against Charles I had been mostly replaced by pro-royalty men. Regicide was bad, kings were necessary, and as long as Charles II was amenable to Parliament, Parliament would sustain the king. As long as the king did not declare war against Parliament the way his father had done, everything would be fine.

But Charles II had seen the days of glory of his grandfather, James I, and his father, Charles I, two unpopular kings who had nevertheless imposed their will. His own position of weakness seemed like subservience to a political body that was supposed to be subject to him. There had to be a way to weaken Parliament.

Charles II found a way. The answer to his dilemma was political parties.

CHAPTER TWO

Charles II was unfortunate to reign at a time when England was beset by one disaster after another. The first of these was the great plague of London, in which a large portion of the population of London expired from the bubonic plague. Charles II moved his royal court out of London into the countryside during this great disaster, leaving the battle against the plague to lesser officials, who buried the dead in huge mass graves dug in the middle of the city. They also imposed other measures, such as killing of all dogs and cats, which scientific minds of the day believed might be spreading the disease. This added an increase in the number of rats and other rodents in the city to the discomforts already being experienced, but, at least, the citizens could be certain that dogs and cats were not spreading the plague. No sooner did the plague subside than the city of London caught on fire and, for the most part, burned to the ground. These misfortunes did not provide Charles II with a favorable economic and political climate for increasing the power of royalty. Charles II was induced into accepting direct bribes from his cousin, Louis XIV of France, in return for helping France with a war against the Dutch and avoiding war against France, the natural enemy of England. It was during these political difficulties that Charles' attention was drawn to two disruptive factions in Parliament which called each other by the derisive names of Whigs and Tories. Whigs was short for Whiggamores, a troublesome group of Scottish separatists. Tories were an infamous band of Irish highwaymen. Whigs in Parliament tended to be nobility and wealthy merchants. Tories tended to be clergy and country gentry. The main question dividing Whigs and Tories concerned the "divine right of kings", as it applied to James, the brother of Charles II, and the person likely to succeed him as king, since Charles II had no legitimate children. Tories supported the divine right of kings. Charles saw it to his immediate advantage to align himself with the Tories, not just because of his brother, but also because of his cousin Louis XIV. An alliance with Tories would help Charles avoid war with France. Whigs questioned the divine right of kings and did not want to see James, an avowed Catholic, ascend to the throne of England.

For a weak and troubled king, the decisions of Charles II have an inordinate effect on governments of today. It was not just his decision to execute the judges who had sentenced his father to death that affected English speaking governments after his time. Even more influential over government today was his decision to select the ministers of his government from a specific party. This was so successful at weakening Parliament that it was written into English law during the reign of Queen Anne, the niece of Charles II.

If Charles II had been a bad king, his successor, James II was a horrible one. With regard to Parliament, James was more like his father than his brother, and this elevated the Whigs into power fairly rapidly. James' daughter Mary, the wife of William of Orange, decided to depose her father, and her husband William arrived in England with an army. Without support from the English people, James II elected to flee to France, leaving his Protestant daughter and her Protestant husband as rulers of England. William, as king of England, at first went through Tory and Whig ministers for his cabinet, but in 1696 appointed a cabinet which was drawn entirely from Whigs. With the deaths, first of Mary and later of William after their successful reign, Mary's sister Anne became queen.

Queen Anne was a high Tory. She replaced most of William's ministers with Tories, but the Whigs held a majority in Parliament. By the end of Anne's reign, Parliament had passed a law requiring the monarch of England to appoint the ministers of the cabinet from the party which held a majority in Parliament. This was the official beginning the two-party corruption that has dominated English speaking governments since that time.

CHAPTER THREE

Despite seventeen pregnancies, Queen Anne died without any heirs to the throne. The Stuarts, the royal family of England, were really putting divine right of kings to the test. Not only had they put together two queens in succession, but now they were completely out of people, except for the little brother of the two queens. However, he had been raised as a Catholic in France, so he was not divine enough to become king of England. The Whigs started calling him The Pretender. It was at this critical juncture that the Whigs unaccountably lost their majority in Parliament. When Queen Anne suddenly died, there was no monarch to replace the Whig ministers still running the government. So while the majority party Tories debated about enthroning James the Pretender, the Whigs went to Germany and located Queen Anne's closest living Protestant relative, a man named George living in Hanover, and declared him king of England. George I had no trouble discerning which side of his bread the butter was on. The Tories were the minority party for the next fifty years, as the Whigs had their way in government, becoming so corrupt that eventually the people of England had enough of them and voted them out of office.

The English people were on their third George, the great-grandson of the first one, when the Whigs were voted out, and the Tories came back into power amid promises of reform and honest government. The problem with reform and honest government when a political party is in power is that it can be very expensive, and any expenses incurred by a political party in power are customarily paid for from public revenues. That is just the way political parties do things. So who should pay for the cost of reform and honest government in England?

Well, one reliable source of public revenues for the British empire was their colonies scattered around the world. Of these, one of the most profitable in the mid-eighteenth century was the American colonies, an established source of revenues for the English government. All that needed to be done was to increase taxes on the American colonies until reform and honest government were accomplished in England. What could possibly go wrong?

So Parliament immediately levied several new taxes on the American colonists, the Stamp Act, the Tea Tax, the Townshend Acts, etc., etc. Job done.

However, the American colonists trashed the Stamp Act offices, threw a shipload of tea into Boston harbor, declared independence from England, and defeated the British military in a war of revolution; all over some taxes that were minute compared to the taxes that American political parties have imposed on Americans of today.

CHAPTER FOUR

The two-party system in England that had resulted in a war of independence in America was a manifestation of a concept that was thought of as essential to European politics, balance of power. Balance of power was an idea that arose from the continual wars that European monarchs waged against each other. The premise was that no one nation should possess sufficient power to subjugate the rest. In practical terms, the people who put this idea into effect were the people who controlled European wealth, the bankers of Europe. If they thought that one nation was becoming too powerful in a war, they would build up the military of the weaker nation, prolong the war, and make money in the process from military contracts, often from both sides of the conflict. Since European monarchs were all related to each other by thinning blood, it was all in the family. War was a family game. Common people were thought of as existing to serve the state. It was the task of royalty to determine which nations would fight each other.

Once American independence was achieved, the prevailing idea in America was that the people of America were the government, and the councils of government existed to serve the people. This idea was particularly adapted to the American colonies, even when they were under British rule, because of the unity of the people at local level. Although there were political parties in the colonial assemblies, they pertained to England more than to the colonies, and once the Revolutionary War started, Tories in America were Americans who still supported England because the Tory Party in England had started the war. During the war and for a considerable time afterward, the goal of Americans was to establish a partyless government, a government in which the sovereignty of the nation belonged to the people, not to a king, and not to any privileged group. With this in mind, Americans wrote the Articles of Confederation, establishing a national government that was too weak to solve most of the problems that arose. Accordingly, delegates from the states met in Philadelphia in 1787 to draft a new Constitution. There was some discussion at the convention of the idea of partyless government, which all of the delegates agreed was a good goal in drafting a Constitution. In the end, they agreed to make no mention of parties in the new Constitution. The preamble to the Constitution shows the concept of government that the framers had in mind, a united people who governed themselves by common consent, the powers of government dependent on the consent of the governed.

Ironically, it was over the question of adoption of the Constitution that the first great political division appeared in the United States, those for adoption being called Federalists, and those opposed being called Anti-Federalists. The arguments of the Federalists prevailed. The Constitution was ratified, and George Washington, who had presided over the Constitutional Convention, was elected the first President of the United States of America, with John Adams as Vice-President.

As his Secretary of Treasury, President Washington chose Alexander Hamilton, one of the leaders of the Federalist movement, and as his Secretary of State, Thomas Jefferson, who was in France when the Constitution was written and adopted. These were the two men largely responsible for the system of two-party corruption that controls the United States today. In a series of events reminiscent of the coronation of Charles II, two political parties started by Hamilton and Jefferson dominated the election of 1800. Independent voters, the voters who had been created by the writing and adoption of the Constitution of the United States, have been prevented from being elected to public office since that time by party control of elections. The idea of partyless government, like the idea of abolishing the office of king in England, existed only briefly in the history of government before it was extinguished. However, there was enough independence in existence during the period between the writing of the Declaration of Independence and the election of 1800 that a Constitution was written that has lasted more than two hundred years.

Both of the first two Presidents spoke out against the formation of political parties. In his Farewell Address, President Washington set forth his ideas about the effect political parties could have on a purely elective government, such as the one the people of the United States had started. Historians of today seem to take the position that Washington was secretly a member of the Federalist Party started by Alexander Hamilton and was insincere about what he said concerning political parties. Where they get that idea, I do not know. It is difficult for me to imagine a way to predict more closely what would happen to the freedoms established in America if political parties came to be supported by the people.

George Washington's comments about political parties are largely ignored today.

"They serve to organize faction, to give it an artificial and extraordinary force, to put in the place of the delegated will of the nation the will of a party, often a small but artful and enterprising minority of the community, and according to the alternate triumphs of different parties to make the public administration the mirror of the ill-concerted and incongruous projects of faction, rather than the organ of consistent and wholesome plans digested by common councils and modified by mutual interests.

"However combinations or associations of the above description may now and then answer popular ends, they are likely, in the course of time and things, to become potent engines, by which cunning, ambitious, and unprincipled men will be enabled to subvert the power of the people, and to usurp for themselves the reins of government, destroying afterwards the very engines which have lifted them to unjust domination.

"Towards the preservation of your government and the permanency of your present happy state, it is requisite, not only that you steadily discountenance irregular oppositions to its acknowledged authority, but also that you resist with care the spirit of innovation upon its principles, however specious the pretexts. One method of assault may be to effect, in the forms of the Constitution, alterations which will impair the energy of the system, and thus to undermine what cannot be directly overthrown. In all the changes to which you may be invited, remember that time and habit are at least as necessary to fix the true character of governments as of other human institutions; that facility in changes, upon the credit of mere hypothesis and opinion, exposes to perpetual change from the endless variety of hypothesis and opinion, and remember especially that for the efficient management of your common interests, in a country so extensive as ours, a government of as much vigor as is consistent with the perfect security of liberty is distributed and adjusted, its surest guardian. It is, indeed, little else than a name, where the government is too feeble to withstand the enterprises of faction, to confine each member of the society within the limits prescribed by the laws, and to maintain all in the secure and tranquil enjoyment of the rights of person and property.

"I have already intimated to you the danger of parties in the State, with particular reference to the founding of them on geographical discriminations. Let me now take a more comprehensive view and warn you in the most solemn manner against the baneful effects of the spirit of party generally.

"This spirit, unfortunately, is inseparable from our nature, having its root in the strongest passions of the human mind. It exists under different shapes in all governments, more or less stifled, controlled, or repressed; but in those of the popular form, it is seen in its greatest rankness and is truly their worst enemy.

"The alternate domination of one faction over another, sharpened by the spirit of revenge, natural to party dissension, which in different ages and countries has perpetrated the most horrid enormities, is itself a frightful despotism. But this leads to a more formal and permanent despotism. The disorders and miseries which result gradually incline the minds of men to seek security and repose in the absolute power of an individual; and sooner or later the chief of some prevailing faction, more able or fortunate than his competitors, turns this disposition to the purposes of his own elevation on the ruins of public liberty.

"Without looking forward to an extremity of this kind, which, nevertheless ought not to be entirely out of sight, the common and continual mischiefs of the spirit of party are sufficient to make it the interest and duty of a wise people to discourage and restrain it.

"It serves always to distract the public councils and enfeeble the public administration. It agitates the community with ill-founded jealousies and false alarms, kindles the animosity of one part against another, foments occasionally riot and insurrection. It opens the door to foreign influence and corruption, which finds a facilitated access to the government itself through the channels of party passions. Thus, the policy and will of one country are subjected to the policy and will of another.

"There is an opinion that parties in free countries are useful checks upon the administration of the government and serve to keep alive the spirit of liberty. This, within certain limits is probably true; and in governments of a monarchical cast, patriotism may look with indulgence, if not with favor, upon the spirit of party, but in those of the popular character, in governments purely elective, it is a spirit not to be encouraged." (Farewell Address, 1796)

One of Washington's purposes in giving this advice was to warn against something that had been taking place within his own administration, a contention between Secretary of Treasury Alexander Hamilton and Secretary of State Thomas Jefferson. Hamilton had aligned himself with New England merchants and manufacturers and sought to advance their interests. As a result, his followers took upon themselves the characteristics of the Whig Party of England, which from its beginning had been comprised of nobility and wealthy merchants. The Whig Party had been less than enthusiastic in its support of the war with the American colonists. Hamilton wanted to have a strong alliance with England based on Whig Party principles. Hamilton's followers called themselves Federalists and did not really consider themselves to be a party until the election of 1800, when Thomas Jefferson and James Madison started the Republican-Democrat Party in opposition to the Federalists.

The Tory Party had caused the Revolutionary War by high taxation. Tories in England were controlled by clergy and wealthy landowners, who also tended to control local administration of justice. By occupation, the Republican-Democrat followers of Jefferson were more like Tories than Whigs and were for the most part, farmers and southern plantation owners. Jefferson and the Republican-Democrats would have been highly insulted to hear themselves compared to the Tories, but there was another similarity which caused the Tories and the Republican-Democrats to be strong parties, while the Whigs and the Federalists were weak parties. The Tory Party was founded on the principle of divine right of kings, which made it the strong party of England.

The sovereignty of the United States is in the people of America, which the Republican-Democrats claimed to represent, while the Federalists were more interested in money and political and economic theory. In all of this, no consideration was made of people who did not join either party. It was just assumed that independent voters had lost their power in government, since the majority of voters had joined political parties.

In comparing American political parties with the English parties they were patterned after, it was the question of slavery that made American parties different from English parties. In England, the Whig Party led out in the abolitionist movement, soon joined by the Tory Party in abolishing slavery in the British empire in 1834. In America the Republican-Democrat Party became the Democratic Party started by Andrew Jackson and Martin van Buren, a pro-slavery party which started the Civil War. The Federalists disbanded and re-organized whenever they became particularly unpopular as National Republicans, Whigs, and finally as Republicans, choosing the right side of the slavery issue and winning the Civil War, but immediately afterward returning to their first great love, money.

The English Whig Party lost control of the English economy and became the English Liberal Party of today. Democrats in America call themselves liberals. The Tory Party became the

Conservative Party and is now the party which controls England's money. Republicans in America call themselves conservatives.

In their imitation of English politics, Republicans can never really become like Conservatives in England because they do not have a monarch. Democrats are the party of popularity. When slavery was popular, they were a strong pro-slavery party. After the Civil War, they aligned themselves with the labor union movement and other organizations of faction resulting from economic and political inequalities, making them today a party with an agenda copied from European socialism.

CHAPTER FIVE

The reasons that Jefferson and Hamilton gave for their political division may seem somewhat irrelevant today, both sides seeming to be antiquated by today's standard. Hamilton was using the power of government to enrich his Federalist friends by clever financial ideas. Almost all of Hamilton's schemes seemed to be at the expense of the farmers and plantation owners who supported Jefferson's party. The original difference still exists in government today.

In 1978 farmers in America were in hard times. Egged on by a farmer's union, farmers from all over America drove their tractors to Washington, D.C., to protest the economic conditions farmers were laboring under and to petition the government for relief. So Washington, D.C., was inundated with tractors clogging up traffic and angering people against farmers, which may have been one reason why government officials refused to listen in any way to these farm tractor protesters. David Stockman, President Reagan's economic advisor, summed up the attitude of Washington, D.C., toward farmers.

If farmers could not follow good business practices, he said, they must face the consequences. So the farmers drove their tractors home minus the money they had spent on fuel to make the trip, and many of them lost their farms to the banks they had borrowed money from.

Contrast that reaction toward farm foreclosures to the house foreclosures of 2008. Bank executives converged on Washington, D.C., in their Lear jets, petitioned the government for relief and left with seven hundred fifty billion dollars, the first of several stimulus packages given directly to banks, some of which immediately used the money for bonuses given to bank executives.

Does it appear that political parties have solved the problem that they used to justify their existence in America?

The bank bailout was supported by both major parties of today. Times have changed. But in 1800 the basic similarity between the two parties was less defined. For one thing, in 1800 all voters were still independent voters. Voters just registered to vote, not as members of political parties. In their opposition to Hamilton's Federalists, Jefferson and Madison hit on the idea of caucuses, the extra-legal use of elected officials for party organization. This idea was so successful that the Federalists were obliterated. It also created a problem in the electoral college that Congress was unable to resolve.

The Republican-Democrats decided to run two candidates for President because under the Constitution, each elector in the electoral college voted for two candidates for President, the candidate receiving the most votes being elected President and the candidate receiving the second most votes being elected Vice-President. This system, which had worked fine in electing Washington and Adams, and then Adams and Jefferson, was not adaptable to party politics. The Republican-Democrats ran Jefferson for President and Aaron Burr for Vice-President, so when Republican-Democrat electors cast their ballots in the electoral college, they all voted for two candidates, Jefferson and Burr, for President. If Republican-Democrats had put any thought into what they were doing one of them would have voted for Jefferson and someone besides Burr, but it did not happen, so there was a tie vote in the electoral college. This threw the election into the House of Representatives to be decided, where Federalist votes went for Burr, and it took thirty-six ballots before Jefferson was finally elected.

Members of Congress considered this to be such a traumatic experience that they decided to make the office of Vice-President an office to be appointed by political parties, rather than an office to be elected by the people, starting the running mate system still in effect today. It is typical of political parties that once the first party candidates were elected, no consideration has been made since that time except the running mate idea they started. The passage of the Twelfth Amendment to the Constitution gave the office of Vice-President to political parties and employed the same reasoning that had split English government into a two-party system, that the political party which prevailed in an election should control the top offices of a nation exclusively. In England this reasoning was used with regard to cabinet ministers; in America it was used with regard to the office of Vice-President.

Congress could have continued on with the kind of elections that had elected Washington and Adams. All they had to do was to give the electoral college or the House of Representatives a better means of breaking a tie vote. They could have said, If there is another tie vote for President, a simple majority in the House can elect the President instead of the two thirds vote now required. It would have taken an amendment to the Constitution, something they had never done, but it took one anyway to change it to appointment by political parties. There was no reason to make it as complicated as they did except that they had been so traumatized by thirty-six votes in the House of Representatives that they could not wait to turn the responsibility for selecting the Vice-President over to political parties. They had accomplished in American government what had been accomplished in English government during the reign of Queen Anne, a law mandating the existence of political parties.

Notwithstanding their success at taking over the government with their political party, Jefferson and his Vice-President were not off to a good start with each other. As it became known to Burr that Jefferson was not going to have him as his running mate in 1804, he decided to run for governor of New York. Due to remarks Alexander Hamilton had made concerning his candidacy for governor, Burr challenged Hamilton to a duel.

After their meeting on the political party field of honor, Hamilton was dead, and Burr was wanted in two states for murder, which did not do a lot for his Vice-Presidency. It was at this point that Burr became interested in an enterprise on the borders of Mexico, which would establish a new nation in which Burr might conceivably get a better job than Vice-President of the United States. Accordingly, Burr and some disaffected persons he had recruited started down the Ohio River on flatboats on their way to some nameless glory. The enterprise collapsed when President Jefferson had them arrested and tried for treason. The Republican-Democrat Party may have secured the office of Vice-President to themselves, but their first Vice-President could scarcely be called a success.

One reason we might want to remember the first political party Vice-President is his fleet of flatboats, probably the first party platform in America.

CHAPTER SIX

If Thomas Jefferson had been told that he was starting a political party that one day would be instrumental in a trillion-dollar bailout of banks at the expense of the taxpayers, he would have thought he was conversing with an insane person. All of the ideals he supported and proposed and that his party stood for were designed to prevent that kind of occurrence in government. The fact is, life under Jefferson's dominating party did not seem so much different from life under independent Presidents Washington and Adams. After all, Jefferson was the man who wrote the Declaration of Independence. He ought to be able to keep the people of the United States independent. The Federalists still existed, but in a severely weakened state, and offered up sacrificial lambs as candidates to be defeated by the Republican-Democrats until the Federalists officially gave up the ghost in 1816, and James Monroe ran unopposed by a Federalist candidate in 1820.

The next election in 1824 resulted in four Republican-Democrat candidates, John Quincy Adams, Andrew Jackson, William Crawford, and Henry Clay, who split the vote, throwing the election into the House of Representatives. John Quincy Adams and Henry Clay combined their support on the promise that Clay would become Secretary of State in the administration of Adams, earning them the election and the everlasting hatred of Andrew Jackson. Adams and Clay then started the National Republican Party, which after a time took the name of Whig Party.

Andrew Jackson won the popular vote in 1824, but lost the election in the House of Representatives. In 1828 the hero of the Battle of New Orleans was ready for his opposition. The National Republican administration of John Quincy Adams had been notable for public works projects, the most prominent of which had been the completion of the Erie Canal in 1825. The election of 1828 was the first election with modern party campaigning. Jackson supporters appeared everywhere with brass bands, electioneering, and party promotion. John Quincy Adams lost the election by a substantial margin.

It was also the election in which the news media took its place as the organ of party propaganda. The election of 1828 is remembered for its mudslinging in the press by both parties.

Once Andrew Jackson was in office, he began to consolidate his followers into a modern political party, changing the name of the party from Republican-Democrat Party to Democratic Party. His greatest help in this effort was his Secretary of State and second Vice-President, Martin van Buren. Jackson and Van Buren were the first American politicians to mount a campaign to convince Americans that political parties were necessary in the United States government, Van Buren even writing a book on the subject. The strength of the Democrats lay in Jackson's personal popularity, organization of faction at local level, and their control over the judicial branch of government, which they used to enforce slavery in the United States. The result was a pro-slavery party that was popular in southern and western states. It was an unfortunate time for such a party to be formed. English political parties had just abolished slavery in the British empire, also giving rise to an abolitionist movement in the United States.

The other thing Jackson did during his Presidency was to mount a campaign against the National Bank. In this campaign Jackson was also successful, breaking the bank and changing United States monetary policy. Jackson is another party politician who would never believe that the party he started gave almost a trillion dollars to banks that were threatening to shut down after the election of 2008.

Perhaps the most significant political party action during the Jackson administration was the action of a minor party, the Anti-Masonic Party, which held the first political party convention and selected William Wirt as its candidate for President. The Democrats were quick to copy this method of selecting a candidate by holding a convention in 1835 and selecting Martin van Buren as their candidate for President and Richard M. Johnson as their candidate for Vice-President.

Martin van Buren was elected President in 1836. His Vice-Presidential candidate, Richard M. Johnson, fell one vote short of having a majority in the electoral college and is the only Vice President to have been elected by the Senate according to the provisions of Amendment XII of the Constitution. The Whigs purposely ran four candidates against Van Buren, hoping to throw the Presidential election into the House. The strategy failed, and Van Buren was elected with a majority of votes in the electoral college. Unfortunately for Van Buren, there was a financial panic in 1837, which the Whigs blamed on Van Buren and Jackson and their campaign against the National Bank.

The Whigs held their first party convention in 1840 and selected William Henry Harrison as their candidate for the Presidency. Harrison defeated Van Buren, but only lived a short time after his election, and his Vice-President, John Tyler, became the first American Vice-President to ascend to the Presidency on the death of a President. The 1840's and 1850's were a period of political indecision between Jackson's strong pro-slavery party and Henry Clay's weak Whig Party, as the dominant political issue became the question of slavery in the United States.

Since political party politicians in America today do little except copy what they see party politicians do in European governments, it is too bad that there was only one weak American party trying to emulate the Whigs and Tories of England during the 1830's. The Democrats of that time were paying more attention to what pro-slavery nations of Europe were doing with regard to slavery than acts of Parliament. Henry Clay's Whig Party was making a half-hearted opposition to slavery, but Clay's idea of opposition was compromise, the Missouri Compromise, the Kansas-Nebraska Compromise, the Compromise of 1850, etc. In the meantime, the British had long since abolished slavery in the British empire. The anti-slavery movement was becoming stronger all the time in the United States, especially in New

England, with no practical means of expression in government under Whig Party and Democratic Party corruption.

Briefly, the 1840's and the 1850's went like this. Democrat James Polk was elected in 1844. Whig candidate Zachary Taylor was elected in 1848. Taylor soon died, and his Vice-President, Millard Fillmore, became President. Democrat Franklin Pierce was elected in 1852, and Democrat James Buchanan was elected in 1856. The Whig Party fizzled out between 1852 and 1856, not even selecting a candidate at its last convention, but voting to support Millard Fillmore, who was the candidate of the American Party. One Whig splinter group started the Republican Party and ran as its candidate the western explorer John Fremont in an anemic first attempt.

By 1860 the anti-slavery elements of the United States had decided to consolidate their efforts by uniting in the Republican Party. This led to the nomination of Abraham Lincoln, who had become the best spokesman for the anti-slavery movement during his unsuccessful campaign against Democrat Stephen A. Douglas for the United States Senate. For the first time in American politics, there was a distinct moral difference between the two prevailing parties. The Democrats were pro-slavery; the Republicans were anti-slavery. The Democrats held a substantial numerical advantage, but a less united front. Given the makeup of the two parties and the condition of the legislative branch of government, there was little possibility of resolving the issue of slavery in a peaceful manner.

The conduct of political parties in pre-Civil War America was in part attributable to the desire to be subject to military leadership. The first strong party leader was a duel fighting, horse racing, hard campaigning, tactical genius military leader who carried his military style into his Presidency and into his campaign against the national bank. If Andy Jackson had slaves, then maybe slavery was not so bad, because one thing was certain, Jackson was a military leader worthy to be Commander in Chief of the United States military. The Whigs were quick to pick up on this attitude and began to nominate war heroes almost exclusively,

William Henry Harrison, Zachary Taylor, and Winfield Scott. The militarism of the time was further heightened by the Mexican War, which the Whig party opposed. Democratic President James Polk started the war, but Whig Generals Taylor and Scott won it.

The two-party system of the United States had become a pro-slavery military discipline going in one direction and a defensive anti-slavery movement going in the opposite direction which would inevitably collide. When the Democrats split their vote in the 1860 Presidential election between Democratic candidate Stephen A. Douglas and a southern Democrat, John Breckinridge, Republican Abraham Lincoln was elected.

In their military manner, seven southern states seceded from the United States during the time between the election of 1860 and the inauguration of Lincoln and declared themselves to be the Confederate States of America. Outgoing Democratic President James Buchanan dithered in the White House wishing that inauguration day would arrive. Upon entering the office of President, Lincoln did not recognize the Confederacy or any right to secede, but seemed to be willing to leave it at that, making no move to force the issue. This made the militaristic Confederates a little impatient, so they attacked Fort Sumter at Charleston, South Carolina, and the Civil War was on.

CHAPTER SEVEN

What was the difference between the government of England and the government of the United States that enabled England to abolish slavery in the British Empire by a vote of Parliament in 1834, while the United States could not abolish slavery thirty years later without a Civil War?

George Washington mentioned in his Farewell Address that sometimes in monarchies political parties can be somewhat justified because they can be the means of opposing unjust administration of government, but there is more to it than that. First, we should talk about rights. The Declaration of Independence, written by slaveowner Thomas Jefferson, said that there are certain inalienable rights, that among these are life, liberty, and the pursuit of happiness. Although Jefferson, as a slaveowner, may have been somewhat hypocritical when he wrote this, he was expressing a group ideal in which some members of the group may have been more in harmony with Jefferson's words than he was himself. In any event, Jefferson did not like slavery, even though he owned slaves until the day he died.

People who were slaves in the United States certainly could see that they did not enjoy the same liberty and pursuit of happiness that non-slaves possessed. But did they actually have a right to these inalienable goals of the founding fathers?

Jefferson said they did, but he did not put it into practice himself. If we are to define rights we need to look at an extreme example. In the last century, an aggressive political party took over most of Europe by military conquest. That party then decided to eliminate a certain group of European citizens from existence and set up extermination camps to accomplish this. So let us consider the rights of the Jews who were being herded into gas chambers at Auschwitz and other extermination camps. Did they have the right to live?

The Nazi Party said they did not. Did that take their right away?

No, their rights to life, liberty, and pursuit of happiness still existed even though they could not exercise those rights because they were being murdered by a political party. As Jefferson stated so eloquently, those rights are inalienable. They belong to all people, however many are denied the inalienable rights that they have.

Secondly, the Constitution of the United States guarantees that there will be liberty and justice for all in the United States. If there is not liberty for all, there is not justice for all, so what caused this breakdown of justice in the United States government?

Once again, we need to consider events that happened in England. When Queen Elizabeth I died, she had named her cousin, King James IV of Scotland, as her successor, so he became King James I of England and Scotland. James I was an unpopular king with his English subjects, and he had similar feelings toward them, especially toward Parliament, a segment of English government he especially did not like. James I began a process of appointing judges to whom he gave the task of "striking down" of acts of Parliament that the king did not like. This caused a Civil War between Parliament and the king during the reign of the next king, Charles I, the son of James I. There were two more Stuart kings after Charles I, Charles II and James II, after which James II was deposed by his daughter Mary and her husband, William of Orange.

In 1689 Parliament declared that James II had abdicated by deserting his kingdom. William and Mary were offered the throne as joint monarchs. They accepted a Declaration of Rights drawn up by Parliament which limited the power of the throne, reaffirmed Parliament's claim to control taxation and legislation, and provided guarantees against the abuses the Stuart Kings had committed. Foremost among the provisions of the Declaration of Rights were two that pertained directly to judges. The Sovereign was not allowed to interfere with elections or free speech, and proceedings of Parliament were not to be questioned in the courts or in any body outside Parliament itself. The King was forbidden to establish his own courts or to act as a judge himself, and the courts were forbidden to impose excessive bail or fines, or cruel and unusual punishments.

In other words, the "striking down" of acts of Parliament that had caused a Civil War and other problems that had been taking place during the reigns of the Stuart Kings was ended. English courts were there to enforce the laws, not to make or change them. All legislative powers were retained by Parliament. The agreement of William and Mary to abide by these terms of the Declaration of Rights made the change in English government that enabled England to outlaw the slave trade in 1807 and to abolish slavery in the entire British empire in 1834. It meant that when Parliament passed a law abolishing slavery, no court could "strike down" what Parliament had done. As soon as parliament abolished slavery, it was unlawful to have slaves in England, and no court of law could change it.

Now we will consider what happened in the United States. The Constitutional Convention put together a government that had all the powers that the English government had possessed plus the advantage of having a President instead of a king. As George Washington clearly advocated, there was no need for political parties in the United States. The government that had been created was capable of solving any problem that might arise. Political parties changed that in a horrific way. It came about in the same election in which political parties kidnapped the office of Vice-President and took it away from the American people.

The election of 1800 generated a Supreme Court case that made it impossible to abolish slavery without a Civil War. If we consider the courts as they existed before 1800, any court in the United States had the power to rule against slavery. The fact that none did except for a Supreme Court decision concerning the slave ship, Amistad, shows the timidity of judges of that time, but essentially any judge was empowered by the Constitution to rule that slavery violated the inalienable individual rights of a person. The state seeking to enforce slavery could then appeal the case, but justice would seem to require that a higher court could just dismiss the case the way they do today when independent voters sue in court trying to regain their right to vote or to be candidates for office. There is nothing that requires a court to be unjust. It is only a tradition among lawyers that it has to be that way. Suppose that a slave had gone to a duly authorized court and said, someone has enslaved me. Please return my freedom to me.

What would the court have done?

First and foremost, judges are lawyers, and lawyers do what lawyers who preceded them did. The slave would have been returned to slavery because what lawyer was going to depart from precedent?

But any of them could have. The Constitution empowered judges in the United States to follow justice, not previous wrong judicial decisions. Notice that in England it took more than a hundred years from the time Parliament established power to legislate abolition of slavery before they actually did it. Today we are in a lot worse circumstances than Americans were in before 1800 because of two hundred years of American injustice.

When Jefferson and Burr tied in the electoral college for President, it took longer to elect and inaugurate a President than in the previous three elections because of the thirty-six votes taken in the House of Representatives. In the meantime, John Adams continued in the office of President until the matter was resolved by the House. Because some judicial offices were being left open by Adams during this period, Congress sent a resolution to Adams advising him to fill these judicial offices for which the Constitution gave him responsibility to appoint. So, John Adams made the appointments. When Jefferson finally assumed office as President, he was upset about these "midnight judges", as he called them. Noticing that some of the appointments had not yet been delivered to the appointees, he directed his acting Secretary of State not to deliver them. William Marbury sued in court to receive his appointment.

When the case reached the Supreme Court three years later, Chief Justice John Marshall handed down the verdict of the Court. The Court ruled that

1. Marbury had the right to sue to receive his appointment.

2. Madison, the Secretary of State, could be compelled to deliver it to him.

3. It was not going to happen because the Supreme Court was "striking down" the act of Congress that had advised the President to make the appointment as unconstitutional.

This Supreme Court decision is pure nonsense on the face of it. The Constitution gives the President the power and responsibility to make appointments of federal judges. The Constitution gives Congress the power to advise the President with regard to anything at all. But more than that it completely ignored the Declaration of Rights that England had adopted in 1689 and reimposed the "striking down" of acts of legislature by the courts that had created such havoc during the reigns of the Stuart Kings.

We have all studied Marbury v. Madison in junior high school. It is the case, we were told, where John Marshall became the greatest judge who ever lived by starting "judicial review". What really happened was that it made Congress practically irrelevant. But, as I mentioned before, members of Congress were the greatest fans of judicial review in existence. It absolved them of all responsibility for anything. If they did anything wrong, it was the responsibility of the Supreme Court to fix it. They could concentrate on increasing taxes on the American people to buy votes to keep themselves in office.

It also made the Republican-Democrat Party a strong political party the same way parties like the Fascists, Nazis, and Communists were strong parties in European governments. The Republican-Democrats were a political party that controlled a judicial system. With regard to slavery, it enabled the Republican-Democrats, later renamed the Democratic Party, to enforce slavery in the United States for the next sixty years.

Once the Supreme Court was stronger than Congress with regard to legislation, there was no way to abolish slavery. The last Supreme Court decision with regard to slavery remains the Dred

Scott decision, in which the Supreme Court upheld slavery in the United States just before the Civil War.

CHAPTER EIGHT

Abraham Lincoln had hoped up until the time Fort Sumter was attacked that war could be avoided. It could have been, but his political party would not allow it. If he had told the seven seceding states, "Well, you have left the United States. Goodbye, and good luck.", then there would have been no war. But the political party policy toward secession had been established while Andrew Jackson was President. South Carolina had voted to nullify a federal law and had threatened to secede from the United States. Consequently, party politicians in the North were already agreed that under no circumstances would a state be allowed to leave the nation once it was a state of the United States.

Militarily, Fort Sumter was of no value to the Union or the Confederacy. In terms of law, if the South attacked the fort, it would be no different from Cuba attacking Guantanamo today. The present Cuban government did not give the United States permission to have a military base at Guantanamo, but they have never attacked it. The truth was that the South thought that they could win a war with the North, much the same as Japan thought they could defeat the United States in World War II. There was a reason for this sentiment. Most of the graduates of West Point were from the South. The best high-ranking officers in the United States military had gone with the Confederacy. The North was left with a skeleton army, while the South filled the ranks of their army with the call, "Come on boys, we are going to defend states rights."

In the end, Lincoln was about the only one defending states rights. The Constitution is very clear about war. Congress shall have the power to declare war. The President shall be Commander-in-Chief of the armed forces. The President issued a declaration after Fort Sumter was attacked declaring that the southern states were in a state of insurrection which would require the United States military to suppress. The declaration called Congress back into session to raise and equip an army of 85,000 to deal with the problem. It was not a declaration of war. Congress has sole power to declare war. Lincoln dealt with the problem this way so that the states in rebellion officially remained part of the United States. Once the war was won, it would be easier to restore them to their previous status in the government. Lincoln's miscalculation was in how difficult it would be to suppress the rebellion. For its part, Congress met and began to raise an army in which the wealthy could pay people less fortunate to take their places in the ranks. Military contracts were awarded to friends and associates of Congressmen, and wormy flour and broken down horses were provided to the new troops.

It took only a few battles with the well-led Confederate army before the Union army was starting to learn the realities of war.

Once the Confederates had the war they wanted so badly, it was only a matter of time before they lost it, as it turned out, a long time. Lincoln elevated a young general named George McClellan to command the army of the Potomac in the East.

McClellan was a brilliant organizer, probably the best person in the nation to overcome the problems of supply originating with a corrupt Congress, one of the reasons he was so popular with his troops. But there were some problems with McClellan. First of all, he was a pro-slavery Democrat, a supporter of Stephen A. Douglas in the election of 1860, differing with the southern Democrats only on the issue of the right of states to secede. Second, he was insubordinate, especially toward General-in-Chief Winfield Scott, who had planned the conduct of the war with what proved to be the winning strategy, a naval blockade of the South and a river based campaign on the Mississippi River designed to split the Confederate states in half. McClellan wanted a campaign with the Confederate capitol, Richmond, as its objective. Conditions became so acrimonious between the two generals that the aged General Scott eventually submitted his resignation to Lincoln, and McClellan was elevated to the position of General-in-Chief, still retaining his command of the Army of the Potomac. This suited McClellan just fine, and he continued to build and train a huge army in the East, but did little with it. He transferred his insubordinate attitude toward the President, making Lincoln wait before receiving him when the President went to see him.

McClellan had only one major engagement with the Confederate army, the battle of Antietam, while Generals Grant and Sherman were making good progress in the west with Winfield's Scott's plan to divide the Confederacy by controlling the Mississippi River. Lincoln replaced McClellan as General-in-Chief with a succession of Union Generals, none of whom could win a battle against Robert E. Lee until Lee made a mistake in tactics against Union General George Meade at the battle of Gettysburg, Pennsylvania, and suffered a major defeat. At this point, Lincoln could see the light at the end of the tunnel and placed General Grant over the army of the east, while General Sherman went into Georgia from the west, and it was only a matter of time before the South had taken enough punishment and decided to surrender.

In the meantime, the election of 1864 took place, in which the Democrats ran pro-slavery military candidate George McClellan against Republican incumbent Abraham Lincoln. Fortunately for America, Lincoln was elected.

On April 15, 1865, President Lincoln was assassinated by a pro-slavery stage actor, John Wilkes Booth.

In the final analysis, there was no one in the United States who could not see that slavery was unjust, from the slaves who suffered under cruel domination to the conspirators who plotted President Lincoln's assassination. The difference was in whether the individual person felt that they personally benefitted in some way from slavery. Some people try to be unjust, others do not.

As it applies to political parties, unjust people tend to want to belong to groups of similar unjust people. This is a manifestation of what President George Washington called "the baneful effects of the spirit of party". Political party members are lazy thinkers, allowing political parties to do their thinking for them. Having set their hearts and minds on a party agenda, they are incapable of taking another course, even to the extreme taken by John Wilkes

Booth and his fellow conspirators after the Confederacy had lost the war.

The effects of the spirit of party were no less evident among the anti-slavery victors of the war. While President Lincoln set forth the best kind of example to the people in his Second Inaugural Address, advocating "malice toward none and charity for all", the Radical Republicans in Congress were in favor of punishment, retribution, and revenge. With the assassination of the President, the Radical Republicans opposed the new President, Andrew Johnson, in every effort he made to follow Lincoln's ideas for reconstruction, finally impeaching Johnson and failing to remove him from office by only one vote.

The result was a reconstruction policy that was based on party corruption, with carpetbaggers from the north descending on Southern states in search of the spoils of war, and scalawags, or southern counterparts in corruption, cheating their own neighbors to share in the dishonesty of the carpetbaggers.

In 1868 Republican candidate Ulysses S. Grant was elected President of the United States and also re-elected in 1872. The Grant administration contained more party corruption than any administration up to that time. It also precipitated a financial panic in 1873, which lasted until 1879. Grant's talent for military leadership did not extend over into his efforts in farming, business, and politics, where he had a tendency to be a failure.

The controversial election of 1876 saw Republican Rutherford B. Hayes elected President over Democrat Samuel B. Tilden by one electoral vote after Tilden won the popular vote. The electoral votes of four states numbering twenty-two votes would go to Hayes. Democrats started calling Hayes by the name of Rutherfraud. For his part, Hayes stated the political sentiment of the time in his campaign slogan, He serves his party best who serves his country best.

This is a little different from George Washington's statement that it is the duty of all Americans to discourage political parties.

In 1880 Republican James Garfield was elected over Democrat Winfield Scott Hancock, two Civil War generals running against one another. Garfield was assassinated by a disappointed office seeker shortly after taking office, and his Vice-President, Chester A. Arthur, became President.

In 1884 Andrew Jackson's "necessary" political party came back into power for the first time since before the Civil War. Democratic candidate Grover Cleveland was elected over Republican James G. Blaine. In 1888 Cleveland won the popular vote, but lost the electoral vote to Benjamin Harrison, the Republican candidate. Cleveland was re-elected in 1892 over Harrison, with 22 electoral votes going to a Populist Party candidate.

In 1896 Republican candidate William McKinley spent five times as much money as his opponent, William Jennings Bryan, who was running as the candidate of two parties. the Democratic Party and the Populist Party. Bryan, for his part, embarked on a speaking tour across the United States. This election was the beginning of modern day politics in which the parties began to raise large amounts of money to promote their candidates in the news media, and the candidates began to openly pay for media exposure. McKinley was elected.

On April 25, 1898, Congress declared war against Spain after the battleship Maine exploded and sank in Havana harbor in Cuba. As a result of this war, the United States obtained the Philippines, Puerto Rico, and Guam. This led to an American-Philippine conflict, during which some of the worst atrocities ever perpetrated by American soldiers took place.

McKinley was re-elected in 1900 after another campaign against Bryan, but assassinated in 1901 by an anarchist, and Theodore Roosevelt, the Vice-President, became President.

As far as the legislative and judicial branches were concerned, suffice it to say that the period of time between the Civil War and the turn of the century was the time when corruption in these two branches of government became a way of life.

CHAPTER NINE

It is not as though American political parties were breaking new ground in government. What they actually did was to make American government the mirror of bad European policy. I have described how the two-party system of political corruption that controls the United States originated in English government. As George Washington described, in monarchical governments political parties can sometimes be the means by which the people can be heard, and so, according to Washington, they could somewhat be justified in European governments, which were almost all monarchies when Washington made his comments. During the 1800's European political parties took two different forms, given the designation of left-wing and right-wing in European politics. Right-wing parties aligned themselves with the nationalism of nations, during this time usually in support of monarchy, while left-wing parties opposed monarchy, often in favor of socialistic or communistic ideals. Germany and Italy were nations that developed strong nationalistic parties during the 1800's, while most European nations had left-wing parties opposed to monarchy.

In 1848 Karl Marx and Friedrich Engels were commissioned by the Communist League of Europe to write a book setting forth Communist ideals. Their book, the Communist Manifesto, called for an overthrow, not only of European monarchy, but also of all wealthy people, called the bourgeois by the Communists. This was to be accomplished by an armed revolution of working class and poor people, who were called the proletariat.

From the left-wing parties of Europe came the labor union movement, a less extreme attempt to improve the lives of the working class in industrial society than Communism, but sometimes also connected to Communism. The labor union movement was also mirrored in American politics during the industrial revolution. The Democratic Party became the party in America aligned with labor unions, while the Republican Party aligned itself with money and wealth once their original goal of abolition of slavery was accomplished by the Civil War. The party alignment with these segments of society actually goes back to the time of Thomas Jefferson and the Republican-Democrats and Alexander Hamilton and the Federalists and has to do with the method each party used to gain support of the voters. The Republicans, like the Federalists from whom they evolved, have always preferred organization of faction through finances, soliciting contributions from wealthy doners to finance party organization. The Democrats, like the Republican-Democrats from whom they came, liked direct organization of faction, creation of dissenting factions which are incorporated into party structure. At the start of the United States, one segment of society excluded from political parties was slaves and minority races, but once slavery was abolished, the Democrats portrayed themselves as the party of the common people, while they portrayed the Republicans as the party of the rich, so most black people today are members of the party that started as a pro-slavery party. The Democratic Party of today likes to present itself as the only voice in government for the disadvantaged.

Political parties in Europe were the antithesis of independence. Whether nationalistic or socialistic in nature, European parties made the people dependent on the state. One thing that made America different was the western states and territories, wide open spaces where there were but few people. In order to encourage settlement of the west, Abraham Lincoln had promoted passage of the Homestead Act of 1862. A person in the United States could claim enough land to make a good sized farm and obtain title to the land by building a livable house and making other improvements within a certain time. Members of Congress from the South had opposed homesteading because it would ensure that western states admitted to the Union would be free instead of slave states. With the beginning of the Civil War and secession of the southern states, Lincoln was able to get the Homestead Act passed, giving Americans an economic and social independence that did not exist in any other country. Americans who felt oppressed in the eastern United States under political party control could get a team and wagon and go west where things were more independent.

The bad thing about this kind of independence was that it made many Americans somewhat apolitical. Leaving a huge group of Americans who did not even vote. The word independent came to be associated with people who did not participate in elections. The Constitution of the United States left it to the states to determine the requirements for political candidacy. While such requirements at first were to just register with state or local governments, as political parties began to gain more control over elections, other requirements were added, such as nomination petition signatures, filing fees, etc., all designed to exclude independent voters from being candidates for office. After a while it was just accepted that independent voters could not be elected to office except in unusual circumstances, such as when political parties had made the people especially angry. Starting with the office of Vice-President, political parties made requirements for candidacy to high offices too difficult for anyone but a party candidate with party backing to be elected. States like North Carolina, which had a high number of independent voters from the beginning, also had high nomination petition signature requirements for independent voters which prevented any independent voters except those who were wealthy enough to meet the requirements to get on the ballot. States with fewer independent voters tended to keep the candidacy requirements lower, since no independent voter was going to be elected anyway,

With the beginning of political party conventions in the 1830's, the division between political parties became more pronounced. It was still up to each individual state to decide the manner and form for registration of its voters. There is still one state, North Dakota, in which voters are not required to register. This points to the difficulty that American political parties had in the beginning in consolidating their power. The ideal situation for political parties is for the state government to require that the voter specify a party preference. At exactly what point and in which states this began to appear is unclear. The modern differentiation into political party designations on the voter registration form seems to have certainly been codified with the start of state primary elections in the 1890's. The spirit of party that divided Americans in the 1800's seemed to have a speculative rather than an administrative origin.

When Americans went to the polls, they wanted to vote for the winning candidate. You would not go to a horse race and bet on the slowest horse. There were some who would vote for an independent or minor party candidate, but not many. The trick to party voting was to belong to a party which would win elections, or, if it lost, could at least say it made a good showing. Minor parties have existed with varying degrees of success in American government, but they have never been able to really challenge the two-party system. The attitude of Democrats and Republicans toward minor parties is entirely different from their attitude toward independent voters. The major parties have never seen minor parties as a threat to major party power, as is seen in the nomination petition signature requirements they give to minor parties. A candidate can run as a minor party candidate with relatively few signatures, whereas, an independent candidate is typically given a signature requirement many times greater than a Democrat or Republican. For instance, in the state where I live, an independent voter running for statewide office has to get 43,000 signatures, whereas, a Democrat or Republican has to get about 7,000. Obviously, independent voters are seen as a threat to two-party corruption.

So far, the two-party system has effectively combatted against any threat to two-party domination. But it is not necessarily a given. The Federalist Party folded up in 1816. The Whig Party went defunct in 1856. The Democrats backed slavery during the Civil War and lost their popularity. The Republicans squandered their Civil War victory by causing a financial crisis in the 1870's. The problem was that in the minds of the people, political parties were the government of the United States. What determined which one would be in power was which one made the least serious mistakes.

The Populist movement at the end of the century brought about a change in party politics that was not for the better. Republican Party leadership did not want anything even resembling Populism to get started in their party. Republican candidates were to be chosen and controlled by Republican Party leaders. Democrats were more open to the idea of candidates coming from the people, but after unsuccessfully running Populist candidate William Jennings Bryan multiple times, they were open to suggestions. Conditions were in place for a major party power consolidation.

The answer was a set of elections to be paid for from public revenues in which the parties would consolidate power behind specific candidates before the general election. This eliminated independent voters from participation in elections in two ways. First, some of these public financed elections were to be closed primaries in which independent voters could not vote, but for which they would have the privilege of financing with their taxes. Second, party primaries gave the appearance that only Democrats and Republicans are real candidates for political office. This was an Europeanization of American political parties which made the twentieth century a century in which independence was declining from start to finish.

Theodore Roosevelt was re-elected in 1904, his Democratic opponent Alton Parker only taking the southern states. Republican William Howard Taft defeated Democrat William Jennings Bryan, who was making his third attempt in 1908, and the Democrats joined the Republicans in putting together the system of primary elections that keeps all but politically elite party members from becoming candidates today. Democrat Woodrow Wilson was elected in 1912 when Teddy Roosevelt started the Progressive Party and split the Republican vote between Taft and him.

On 28 June 1914 the Archduke of Austria was assassinated by a Serbian extremist, starting World War I.

CHAPTER TEN

As anyone who has studied European history might expect, the assassination of the Archduke of Austria by a Serbian ended up as a war between Germany and the United States. First Austria, Hungary, and Germany were fighting Serbia and Russia. Then Germany was fighting England and France. Then a German U-boat sank an American passenger ship, and the Americans had to send troops to Europe to win the war. Then the Germans surrendered without Germany being invaded, causing German Corporal Adolf Hitler to believe that somewhere in the High Command, Germany had been betrayed.

The Russians had a particularly bad time of it in World War I. They lost about a million soldiers fighting the Germans for Czar Nicholas II. Then there was a Communist revolution, the Bolsheviks killed the Czar and his family, and Russia became the Union of Soviet Socialist Republics.

With the War to End All Wars completed, President Wilson started the League of Nations, but could not get Congress to authorize the United States to join.

In the election of 1920, Republican Warren G. Harding defeated Democratic candidate James G. Cox in a landslide. The Harding administration has the distinction of having the second most high ranking government officials of any administration end up in prison. To say that the Harding administration was corrupt is an understatement. Harding died from a heart attack in 1923 and was succeeded by Vice-President Calvin Coolidge. Coolidge was re-elected in 1924. Republican Herbert Hoover won a landslide victory against Democrat Al Smith in 1928.

During the 1920's the machinations of American political parties, while they may have seemed important to many Americans, were of little consequence in shaping the events to come. American political parties had tied themselves to European politics, and it was three European political parties that would control the fate of the world for most of the remainder of the century. The first of these was the Communist Party, the party which arose from the writings of Karl Marx and which openly advocated revolution, overthrow of capitalism, and an eventual worker's paradise which could only be achieved under world Communism. The Soviet Union had resulted from an overthrow of the Czarist government of Russia, the first of what Communists hoped would be many Communist revolutions. Communism was the extreme left wing of European politics.

The other two significant parties were the Fascist Party in Italy, which came into power in 1921 and whose leader, Benito Mussolini, shared power with the Italian king, Victor Emmanuel III. This was a party that was promoted in a mystical way as a recurrence of the glory of the Roman Empire. By itself, it would probably never have amounted to much, but it helped bring into power another party in Europe which did become a significant force. That was the National Socialist Party of Germany, later known as the Nazi Party.

The National Socialists were a small socialist party which had the misfortune to be joined by a young former German soldier named Adolf Hitler. Hitler soon learned that he had a talent for making political speeches, and starting with his belief that Germany had been betrayed at the end of World War I, he was soon the dominant personality of the party. It was at this time that Hitler noticed the Fascist Party, which had just come into power in Italy, and patterned his party organization and path to power after what the Fascists had done. It did not work for Hitler's party, and Hitler ended up in jail.

Hitler's year in jail gave him time to organize his thoughts and write a book. After his release from incarceration, the organization of faction within his party was based on three primary things, anti-Semitism, anti-Communism, and German nationalism. The collapse of the German economy during the worldwide economic depression after 1928 brought Hitler's Nazi Party into power. The Depression resulted in two huge political parties in Germany, the Communist Party and the Nazi Party. Since the Communist Party required a revolution to take control of the government, the Germans chose to elevate the Nazis, and German Communists ended up without a party, employed in supporting the German war effort.

CHAPTER ELEVEN

When the stock market crashed in 1929, Herbert Hoover should have been the best qualified person in America to deal with the problem. During World War I, Hoover was leader of war relief in Europe, distributing food, clothing, and other necessities to victims of the war. After the war he was Secretary of Commerce in the administrations of Presidents Harding and Coolidge, dealing with disasters such as the great Mississippi River flood in 1927. But as unemployment skyrocketed, the President seemed paralyzed, the government immobilized by a deadlock between a Republican President and his Democratic Congress. In 1932 the people elected Democratic candidate Franklin D. Roosevelt in a landslide.

Roosevelt was re-elected in 1936. Progress in America against the Great Depression was slow. By 1939 unemployment was at about 10%, down from 24% in 1933, but still not good. However, the predominating political party in the 1930's was the Nazi Party of Germany. Runaway inflation brought an end to the German Weimar Republic and brought the Nazi Party into power. Hitler was appointed Chancellor of Germany in 1933. From this appointive office, Hitler maneuvered himself into the position of absolute dictator of Germany when the aged President of the German Weimar Republic, Paul von Hindenberg, died. Once in control of Germany, the Nazi Party employed the people in public works projects, persecution of Jews, and rearmament of Germany. The Axis Alliance of Germany and Italy eventually took over almost all of Europe by force.

Compare what happened in Germany to President George Washington's analysis of the effect political parties could have on elective governments, made in 1796.

"The disorders and miseries which result gradually incline the minds of men to seek security and repose in the absolute power of an individual, and sooner or later the chief of some prevailing faction, more able or more fortunate than his competitors, turns this disposition to the purposes of his own elevation, on the ruins of public liberty."

This was not the first time democratic ideals had become absolute dictatorship in Europe. The French Revolution had resulted in Emperor Napoleon Bonaparte and his attempt to conquer the world. The Nazi dictatorship was a particularly horrific dictatorship because of the attempt of the Nazis to exterminate all Jews in Europe.

In 1936 Japan was added to the Axis Powers by treaty. Two years later Japan drew the United States into World War II with an attack on United States naval forces at Pearl Harbor, Hawaii.

In 1936 Democratic incumbent Franklin Roosevelt defeated Republican Alf Landon in a landslide and again in 1940 Roosevelt defeated Republican Wendell Willkie. After Roosevelt defeated Thomas Dewey in the 1944 election, the 22nd Amendment was added to the Constitution, limiting a United States President to two terms in office. Roosevelt died from a cerebral hemorrhage on April 15, 1945, and Harry S. Truman became President. Fifteen days later Adolf Hitler committed suicide in his bunker in Berlin, as Soviet troops neared his position. British and United States troops were advancing from the other direction through western Germany. President Truman ended the war with Japan by destroying two Japanese cities with atomic bombs in August of the same year. World War II resulted in about 60 million deaths, one third of which were military deaths and two thirds civilian deaths. Included in the civilian deaths were six million Jews who were killed in Nazi concentration camps.

CHAPTER TWELVE

As we have seen, the Fascist Party and the Nazi Party did not provide their members with good leadership, even though they did all of the things that political parties do. They organized faction, they enfeebled the public administration, they initiated incongruous projects of faction, they elevated persons instead of principles of government, and they destroyed the liberty of the people. We shall now consider the other great party of Europe, the Communist Party, which had its origins in the industrialized nations of western Europe, but first overthrew the eastern and less industrialized nation of Russia. The next Communist revolution began in the non-industrialized nation of China, but it was put on hold while both sides fought the Japanese in World War II. After the war, the Communists finished taking over China. Russia had overrun many Eastern European countries in defeating the German army, and those overrun countries automatically became Communist satellite nations.

Finally, Communist North Korea moved its army into South Korea and drove the South Korean army and Americans in South Korea to the very southern tip of the Korean peninsula. President Truman ordered General Douglas McArthur to move American troops from occupied Japan into Korea, and the Korean Conflict was on. The Korean Conflict began in 1950. Harry Truman had defeated Republican Thomas Dewey in the election of 1948. The Korean Conflict ended in a stalemate at the 38th parallel after Communist China entered the war on the side of North Korea. The Korean Conflict was the first of many undeclared wars engaged in by the United States after World War II, the last time Congress declared war.

The Soviet Union had tested its first nuclear weapon in 1949, having learned how to make the device from Communist spies who worked on the American project to make the first atomic bomb. The United States and Russia engaged in a nuclear arms race throughout the 1950's and 60's, producing enough nuclear weapons to destroy all life on earth several times.

Republican Candidate Dwight D. Eisenhower defeated Democrat Adlai Stevenson in 1952 and again in 1956. In 1959 Fidel Castro led a Communist overthrow of the government of Cuba.

Democrat John F. Kennedy defeated Republican Richard M. Nixon in 1960 for the Presidency. Kennedy encouraged a CIA led invasion of Cuba by Cuban refugees which was unsuccessful. The next year pictures taken by a United States spy plane showed that Russian ICBM missiles were being brought into Cuba. President Kennedy ordered a blockade of Cuba until the missiles were removed. President Kennedy was assassinated in November of 1963 in Dallas, Texas, by Lee Harvey Oswald, and Lyndon B. Johnson, the Vice-President, became President. Johnson was re-elected in 1964 against Republican candidate Barry Goldwater.

When Johnson became President, there were 10,000 American military advisors in South Vietnam helping the South Vietnamese against a Communist insurgency. Johnson increased the number of Americans to a total of 550,000 without a declaration of war. Eventually, Americans were suffering more than 1,000 casualties per month.

The Civil Rights movement during Johnson's Presidency resulted in the Civil Rights Act of 1964 and the Voting Rights Act of 1965. Republican Richard M. Nixon defeated Johnson's Vice-President, Hubert Humphrey, in the election of 1960. Nixon immediately opened peace talks with the North Vietnamese to end the Vietnam War. A cease fire was declared, and United States forces were withdrawn in 1973. But the re-election of Nixon against George McGovern in 1972 resulted in the Watergate scandal and Nixon's resignation in 1974, as he was replaced by Speaker of the House Gerald Ford. North Vietnam then broke the cease fire and overran the South Vietnamese army, taking South Vietnam in 1975.

Democrat Jimmy Carter defeated Republican Gerald Ford in 1976. The Carter administration is remembered for poor economic times and for Americans held hostage in Iran. Carter was defeated by Republican Ronald Reagan in 1980.

The hostages were released, the economy improved, and a deranged man attempted to assassinate the President. Reagan was re-elected by a landslide in the election of 1984 against Democrat Walter Mondale. Reagan's second term started well with one on one talks with Soviet leader Mikhail Gorbachev, resulting in an agreement to reduce nuclear weapons and, eventually, to the end of the Cold War. The latter part of Reagan's second term became embroiled in the Iran-Contra affair. Reagan learned that he was suffering from Alzheimer's disease before his second term ended.

Reagan's Vice-President, George H. W. Bush, was elected in 1988 over Democrat Michael Dukakis. In 1990 and 1991 the Mother of all Battles was fought in Kuwait after Iraq invaded that country, and American troops in Operation Desert Storm drove the Iraqis back into Iraq. George H. W. Bush was defeated in the election of 1992 by Democrat Bill Clinton.

During the early 1990's, Yugoslavia, the pride of European socialists, and the nation which had been held up to the world as how socialism could benefit a nation, erupted into civil war. First, the Serbs were fighting the Croats, then the Serbs started mass homicides of Bosnian Muslims and Albanians in Kosovo. President Clinton sent the American military to bomb the Serbs and stop the genocide.

Clinton was re-elected in 1996, defeating Republican Bob Dole. Clinton was impeached during his second term for obstruction of justice, but not convicted by the Senate.

Republican George W. Bush, son of President George H. W. Bush, was elected in 2000 against Democrat Al Gore in an election that was decided by the United States Supreme Court in a case involving disputed votes in the state of Florida. In 2001 the twin towers of the World Trade Center in New York City were destroyed by a terrorist attack, killing 2750 people. The President then sent United States troops to fight Al Qaeda and Taliban Muslim extremists in Afghanistan after it was determined that the suicide terrorists who had brought down the twin towers were trained by Al Qeada terrorists protected by Taliban leaders in Afghanistan. American troops were later sent into Iraq. George W. Bush defeated Democrat John Kerry in the election of 2004. Democrat Barack Obama, the first African American President of the United States, was elected in 2008 against Republican John McCain after an economic crisis in the last year of George W. Bush's Presidency. Obama was elected to a second term over Republican Mitt Romney.

The election of 2016 was one of the most acrimonious in United States history. The Democrats had a candidate they felt could not fail to be elected. Hillary Clinton had been First Lady of the United States, Senator from New York, and Secretary of State in the Obama administration. Democrats were going to break the glass ceiling by electing a woman to be President. Her Republican opponent was Donald Trump, a wealthy businessman whose only previous political experience had been as a member of the Democratic Party, who happened to notice that he could gain a following among Republican voters if he claimed to be a pro-life Republican and organized opponents of abortion with a Democratic Party style organization of faction. One problem with the Republican candidate's candidacy was his former lifestyle as a Democrat voter, which enabled his Democrat opponents to expose some of the more salacious scandals of his past life. But the Democratic candidate was not without problems of her own, which the Republican propaganda machine also made great noise about. So after the dirtiest Presidential campaign in history, Republican Donald Trump was elected with a majority of votes in the electoral college after losing the popular vote. Angry Democrats kept up a campaign in the news media against Trump throughout Trump's Presidency, also impeaching him twice in the House of Representatives, but failing to get the two-thirds vote in the Senate necessary to convict him. A worldwide corona virus epidemic occupied the nation during the last year of Trump's Presidency.

The election of 2020 should have shown Americans that Democrats and Republicans are too far apart in terms of party contentions to ever resolve the differences between them. Democrat Joe Biden was elected by a small margin, causing Trump supporters to riot at the Capitol on January 6, 2021, as the vote for Biden was being certified by Congress. The Biden administration has been plagued from its beginning with inability to deal with a crisis of illegal immigration at the southern border, an inept withdrawal from the Afghanistan War that allowed billions of dollars' worth of military weapons to fall into the hands of the Taliban, and a war in Ukraine between Ukraine and Russia that the Democrats seem to be determined should involve the United States.

If we should have learned anything from more than two hundred years of party control, it should be that George Washington was correct when he said that political parties have a bad effect on governments that have elections, and that they are incapable of providing good government.

CHAPTER THIRTEEN

We need to start discussing elections because that is where the solution to bad government lies. Obviously, political parties are not giving us good elections because after the election of 2016 Democrats talked about nothing else but election interference, which they claimed had been orchestrated by Russia and Donald Trump. In like manner, Trump supporters claimed that the election of 2020 was won by Democrats through election fraud and use of the news media and social media on the internet to exclude Republicans from getting their message to the voters. But the Republicans, even though they mounted a massive campaign in the courts between election day and the inauguration of Biden to contest the election in the courts, failed to get even one court to hear their complaints.

Independent voters have known for a long time that taking complaints about elections to the courts is a waste of time. I have done it myself. I filed in federal court for relief from the excessive nomination petition signature requirement for independent voters in this state. Federal district court refused to hear the case, citing case law that says that a state may require proof of a "modicum of support" before placing a candidate on the ballot. The question that remains is that if 43,000 signatures are proof of a "modicum of support" for an independent candidate, why are Democrat and Republican candidates not required to show proof of a "modicum of support"?

Their signature requirement to run for the same offices is about 7,000 signatures, one sixth of the proof of a "modicum of support" that an independent is required to show. Republicans now complain about a two-tiered justice system, but it is actually a three-tiered justice system. There is one set of rules for the strong Democratic Party, another stricter set of rules for the weak Republican Party, and still another for independent voters. One thing that the Republicans seem to have learned from these last elections is that the Democratic Party has controlled the judicial system of the United States since 1803. Republicans are not going to be any more successful in resolving complaints about elections in courts than independent voters have been. Their party is too weak. Democrats are going to continue to say that the worst crime in the United States is to question an election won by a Democrat.

It is not as though there is no proof that Democrats in the past have engaged in election fraud. Before the Civil War, as a result of the Kansas-Nebraska Act, the territories of Kansas and Nebraska were added to the United States. The idea was that Nebraska would be a free territory, and Kansas would be slave. But an influx of migrants from the midwest into Kansas territory tipped the balance of voters in favor of a free territory. So pro-slavery Missourians infiltrated the election for the territorial legislature of Kansas, voting in Kansas and electing a pro-slavery legislature. Upon discovering what pro-slavery Missourians had done, the citizens of Kansas held another election and elected a free territory legislature. Supporters of these two contending legislatures in Kansas territory began warring between themselves, earning Kansas the title of "Bloody Kansas". It was in this precursor to the Civil War that John Brown became famous as an abolitionist contender. Whether they are on the right or wrong side of a party contention, political party activists always seem to want to take their contention too far. John Brown attacked the federal arsenal at Harper's ferry. Trump's supporters rioted at the Capitol in Washington, D.C. Democrats spent the entire summer of 2020 rioting all over the United States, causing numerous deaths and billions of dollars in property damage. The only people in the United States who seemed inclined to be law abiding citizens as a political group were independent voters. So we might want to comment on independent voters, their place in American government, and what they can do in the future because, unless Democrats and Republicans can show a riot organized by independent voters, this segment of American society seems to have a better plan for the future than political parties have.

In 2009, for the first time since 1800, there were more Americans claiming to be independent voters than Democrats, the largest political party in America since that election. This is a landmark in American politics that is significant, even though both major parties are pretending it did not happen. To show how it is significant, we need to examine voter registration in one state, Arizona, because Arizona shows why independent voter registration will continue to increase, while the two-party system will continue to decrease in popularity.

In 1988 all deputy registrars in Arizona who were registered independent were dismissed and informed that they were no longer eligible to serve in that position. Deputy registrars were persons who were trained by County Recorders to register voters and authorized by the state to perform that function. Political party leadership had become concerned because in the election of 1986, for the first time in state history, independent voters had started to become deputy registrars. Most of these resulted from the candidacy of an independent candidate for governor of Arizona. The immediate cause of the dismissal was a House bill in the Arizona legislature, which was signed into law by Governor Rose Mofford, requiring that deputy registrars in the state of Arizona be recommended by the chairman of a political party. After December 31, 1988, there were no longer any deputy registrars in Arizona who were registered independent.

As the forty-eighth state admitted to the Union, Arizona was a little deeper into party control than some states. In 1988 Arizona had about 200,000 independent voters who were prevented from voting in party primaries by closed primary elections. The majority of people in Arizona took great pride in not even being registered to vote, voter registration in 1988 standing at 48% of those in Arizona who were eligible to vote. Independent deputy registrars did not appear to the leadership in either party to fit into their system of voter registration, especially with more than half the state not registered to vote. It was something for the state legislature to correct.

Usually this kind of political action went unnoticed. This time it did not. An independent voter in Glendale, Arizona, filed a lawsuit seeking re-instatement of independent deputy registrars. When the date for that court case approached a few years later, the two major parties took a surprising action. Evidently not wanting to discuss voter registration in court, they passed a bill in the legislature, signed into law by Governor Fife Symington, doing away with the position of deputy registrar altogether in the state of Arizona, nullifying the court case. When this law went into effect, it became possible for any person to go to a County Recorder, obtain voter registration forms, and register voters. Why the politicians of the state thought that making it possible for illegal aliens, convicted felons, and foreign nationals to register voters was preferable to having a few independent voters serving as deputy registrars was never explained.

In any event, the new law required a new voter registration form because the signature of a deputy registrar was no longer required to validate a voter registration. Secretary of State Betsey Bayless made up the new voter registration form and sent it to the Justice Department in Washington, D.C. for approval. The new voter registration form had a feature that had an unusual effect on voter registration, one that party politicians did not foresee or even notice for some time. Next to the space marked Party Preference, the Secretary of State had placed a little check box marked None. People registering to vote in Arizona marked that little check box so often during the next ten years that Arizona became the state with the highest rate of independent voter registration in the country.

By 1998 there were enough independent voters in the state to pass an initiative for open primary elections. This presented a puzzle for Arizona politicians. It was plain for them to see that they had shot themselves in the foot. This would require a little creative politics. First, they moved the Presidential Primary election from August to February, leaving the primary election for state offices in August. Independent voters would get to help pay for two primary elections instead of just one...Then Arizona State Attorney General Janet Napolitano provided an opinion that independent voters were not eligible to vote in the Presidential Primary held in February because the Presidential Primary had not been mentioned by name in the Open Primary Initiative. This was an example of the blatant government of the parties, by the parties, and for the parties employed by political party politicians against independent voters at state level. The other foot came down on independent voters when the Libertarian Party obtained a judgment in Federal District Court to prevent independent voters from voting in the Libertarian Party Primary in Arizona. The Open Primary initiative had in effect been totally nullified.

Party leaders in Arizona had hoped that nullifying the Open Primary would discourage citizens of Arizona. Instead, it seemed to have the opposite effect. Independent voter registration started to go exponential. It was at this point that Republican leaders suddenly discovered that illegal aliens could register to vote. In fact, illegal aliens could register illegal aliens to vote because party politicians had done away with deputy registrars in the early 90's. So Republican leaders drew up an initiative called Proposition 200, which they said would stop illegal aliens from registering to vote and worked the news media and talk radio in Arizona into a state of frenzy. The voters approved Proposition 200. The initiative then went to the legislature, where a Senate bill was drawn up requiring a new voter registration form, the wording of which was taken verbatim from Proposition 200. It was signed into law by Governor Janet Napolitano in April of 2005. But, in fact, it did nothing to stop illegal voter registration except to require voters to show identification at the polls. The only real change in the Arizona voter registration form was removal of the little check box to be checked by persons registering as independent voters.

So, once again, the Secretary of State of Arizona sent a voter registration form to the Justice Department in Washington, D.C., to be approved, and the new voter registration form went into effect in September of 2005. In November of the same year a Republican Party spokesman in Pinal County, Arizona, spilled the beans about the real reason for Proposition 200.

"In the 2004 gubernatorial election, Democrat candidates were required to obtain 4,037 signatures, while Republicans had to collect 4,602 to earn a spot on the ballot. Independents, however, were forced to collect more than three times as many signatures—a whopping 14,692—to make the ballot.

The numbers are based on a percentage of registered voters statewide. Independents account for nearly 25% of all voters, a number that's up seven percent since 2000 and continually increasing.

"However, Bill Bridwell, President of the Western Pinal Republican Club, feels that increase in independents is misleading and is the result of a voter registration form created by former Secretary of State Betsey Bayless. The form had a box for voters to check for no party preference. If they wanted to register as Republicans or Democrats, they had to actually fill in a blank.

"'The independent growth trend, in my opinion, is not as large as it would appear………This huge growth of the independent voters occurred from the time that voter registration form was issued until three months ago when a new form was created. We are finding they are now declaring themselves to be Democrat or Republican. It's likely those numbers aren't going to continue to grow like they had for the previous three or four years.'

"Bridwell also feels independent voters don't play a significant role in Arizona politics.

"'While there's a large block of independent voters, they haven't shown up in the polls. It still is as it always has been, a two-party system in Arizona. If you are not a major party candidate, there is no large block of voters that will turn out for you…. If they were significant they would have had an impact in the last two election cycles. When you look at the numbers, they just aren't there.'"

Mr. Bridwell was not just making an idle boast. The rate of independent voter registration in Arizona did decrease.

2000-2002	107,715
2002-2004	165,771
2004-2006	26,384

If independent voter registration had decreased to zero, it might have meant something. As it was, independent voter registration decreased from 80,000 per year to 13,000 per year and then began to rise again as Arizona voters discovered that they could still register as independent voters. By 2008 it was back up to 40,000 per year. Political parties in Arizona had done their best and accomplished nothing. Independent voters passed Democrats in numbers in 2009 and passed Republicans in 2012. The Trump phenomenon put Republicans ahead again, but Arizonans are really fairly independent minded. One of their two Senators noticed the number of independent voters in the state and changed her voter registration from Democrat to independent, partly because the Democratic Party kept trying to tell her she had to vote the party line.

CHAPTER FOURTEEN

It is not to be expected that political parties and their corrupt politicians are going to see the error of their ways and suddenly repent of the evil they have done. They are going to see the error of their ways and attempt to stay in power. They are going to use every unfair advantage, every dishonest practice, every form of dishonesty, all of the public revenues they can lay their hands on, and all of the power of public administration to try to stay where they are.

Independent voters, having arrived at the point they now occupy, need to be realistic about their government. It is controlled by self-created societies. There are a couple of ways to weaken what George Washington called the "artificial authority" of political parties. The first is voter registration. Independent voters are doing well in this capacity, I think the reason for this is a lesson learned from the Civil War in 1860. When Andrew Jackson and Martin van Buren promoted the Democratic Party as being "necessary" in American government, the success of their effort reduced the number of independent voters in the government to such a small percentage that there was no alternative to the contentions of the Democrats and Republicans. Independent voters did not even enter into the equation because there were so few of them. The situation is different today. The number of independent voters began to increase nationwide after the assassination of John F. Kennedy. Americans were not in favor of contentions that rise to the level of killing the President. Although independent voters were prevented from voting in some of the elections they paid for and had no practical means of being candidates for political office, they gradually gained enough numbers through voter registration so that, whether political parties are willing to admit it or not, independent voters now affect elections because political party candidates must do well with independent voters in order to be elected. Candidates who become too contentious or oppressive lose the support of independent voters, who registered as independents because they wanted out of the mindless arguing of party politicians. Who knows what the level of contention would be today if there were not more independent voters than Democratic Party members, who constitute the largest political party in America?

By itself, registration of independent voters has the capacity to bring down the two-party system. If party politicians are to win the votes of independent voters, they have to keep their irrationality within certain limits. What is clear is that party politicians do not have the ability to stop independent voter registration. It is not from lack of trying. There are states that have passed legislation to require party membership. It never lasts very long. People always want to be independent voters. As I mentioned before, independent voters have a Constitutional origin to their existence. Political parties do not. Political parties are self-created societies. If we want to be technical, however powerful political parties may become in the United States, they are independent citizens of the United States who have subjected their freedom to political parties, which, according to George Washington, should not even be there.

I once read an account of pre-World War II Nazi Germany which described Hermann Goering driving his sports car through traffic in downtown Berlin while members of the public looked on and admired the spectacle he presented, a man who obviously seemed to have his life in order. Political parties and political party leaders attract this kind of admiration. But it is not really good government. Popularity in popular government does not always result in accomplishment of what needs to be done.

The second way to break the "artificial authority" of political parties is independent candidates for public office. Political party politicians habitually refer to independent candidates as "third party" candidates. Independent voters are not a political party. They are United States citizens who are registered to vote. When the United States began, that was all that was thought of as being necessary in order to participate in government. With regard to certain political offices, there may be other requirements. For example, in order to be eligible to serve as President, a person must be a natural born citizen, at least thirty-five years of age, and have been at least fourteen years a resident of the United States. Political parties have no right to say that only members of two corrupt political parties are eligible to hold this office. But that is what they do, along with most other political offices in the United States.

What independent voters should keep in mind is Washington's warning against starting political parties, meaning that all candidates for office should be independent candidates, and voters should heed Washington's advice and not support political party candidates. The problem that exists right now is that there are no independent candidates. All independent voters should consider registering as independent candidates. Independent candidates do not have to be elected in order to change the government for the better. All independent candidates have to do is exist.

Party politicians are fond of saying that if a voter does not vote for a Democrat or Republican, they have wasted their vote. My personal belief is that if a voter votes for a candidate they do not really want in office, they have wasted their vote. The two-party system puts up some really sorry political candidates, especially in recent elections. They seem to get worse every succeeding election. I have a tendency to vote for independent candidates who have no chance of being elected just because I think the major party candidates are so unqualified to hold office.

The truth of the matter is that almost all of the people you see today running as independent candidates are really political party personalities who lost a primary election, fell into disfavor with a political party, or had an excessive amount of money they decided to use in an independent candidacy, political party candidates running in independent candidacies, just as Aaron Burr did before killing Alexander Hamilton. A true independent candidate would say that independent candidacy is the correct way to run for public office, while political party candidacy is an incorrect way copied from European governments.

In the European Union today there are only some political parties recognized as having the right to participate. The two major parties carry that attitude into American politics, moving in state governments from time to time to eradicate minor parties. In Arizona the State Attorney General eliminated all minor parties in the state except the Libertarians several years ago for failure to file the excessive paperwork the major parties require political parties to file every year.

The two major parties today believe that the voters are property of the two major parties. Both major parties are now pro-slavery, with only the major parties having the right to own slaves. The Democratic Party has regarded independent voters as slaves to their party since their party began.

The way for Americans to break out of this stranglehold is for ordinary Americans to register as independent candidates for office, especially for state and local offices, where they have the best chance of getting on the ballot. The majority of voters are still party members. Party members vote for party candidates. They practice voting year around in gambling casinos and other places where there are games of chance. The goal of the political party voter is to vote for the winning candidate. Many of the voters who are registered as independent voters are, in fact, political party voters. We need to respect the right of all Americans to vote the way they choose to vote. It is unlikely that any independent voter at the present time is going to register as a candidate, become known to the voters by unbiased coverage in the news media, and be elected on election day. Party controlled elections do not work that way. First of all, party politicians take unimaginable amounts of money from public revenues and give it directly to the news media in return for exclusive coverage of political party candidates. That is the way the system works. The public is unlikely to ever know that an independent candidate is running for office. Secondly, the nomination petition signature requirements for independent candidates in many states are far beyond the capacity of most Americans to meet.

Go register as a candidate and start getting signatures anyway. Candidates for office can usually gain some capacity for registering voters. An independent candidate in these times should be working to increase the number of independent voters, not worrying about getting elected. Independent voters and independent candidates have to look at the realities.

Suppose that a college student registers as an independent candidate for the state legislature. In Arizona that candidate could then go to a County Recorder and obtain two hundred voter registration forms. So could anyone else, but why would anyone else do it?

An independent candidate in Arizona has to get about six times as many signatures to get on the ballot as a Democrat or Republican, but it may be within reach for a state office.

About three out of four students will say, "Sorry, not registered to vote."

Even a political science student could figure out what to do with the two hundred voter registration forms after a while. Once the two hundred forms are gone, the County Recorder will give the candidate another two hundred.

College campuses are the best places to register voters because most college students are not registered to vote, and they are more likely to register independent than anyone else. If independent voters are smart, they will not emulate political party voter registration. When I first registered as a voter in Arizona, I had to sit through a lecture by a deputy registrar about how Arizona had a closed primary, and an independent voter could not vote in the primary election. The best way to register voters is to just register them the way they say they want to register. Given current trends, there will be more independent voters than Democrats or Republicans.

The reason why independent voters need to start registering voters is because political parties are so incapable at this particular thing. Even with the wide-open voter registration

Arizona now has, voter registration has gone up but little since 1988, when 48% of those eligible were registered to vote. The reason for the slight increase is that it is much easier to register to vote now.

CHAPTER FIFTEEN

The kind of government we have depends on two things, voters and candidates for office, the two things that political parties try to limit and eliminate in government, leaving only their corrupt candidates to be approved by party voters. Party controlled elections are not free and open elections, the kind of elections required by the Constitutions of most of the states. We will know we are having free and open elections in the United States when independent candidates are running against independent candidates and being elected.

Obviously, that is going to take some amount of time, since there are but few independent voters running as candidates for office at the present time, and if there are any, the news media makes certain that the voters do not know anything about them.

So, what views should independent voters represent?

An independent voter is a United States citizen registered to vote. United States citizens are allowed to have whatever political beliefs they want to have, including the desire to be subject to self-created societies. We might define political party members as independent voters who have traded their freedom and independence for the ability to be subject to political party platforms, agendas, and regimentation. With a news media paid to give party candidates exclusive promotion in the news, voters have no idea what individual independent candidates stand for. That is an obstacle that will have to be overcome. Right now, individual independent voters need to register as candidates for public office, whatever their personal beliefs or political philosophies. They need to do it in order to register more independent voters, not with the expectation to immediately be elected to office. If enough independent voters register as candidates, some will be elected.

If independent voters take this attitude toward elections, they will break the power of the two major parties fairly rapidly because there will be a great contrast between political party candidates and independent candidates. Independent candidates can be ordinary Americans who register as candidates, solicit no money from the voters, make no expenditures, seek no publicity, and who improve the government by registering voters. Speaking for myself, if I went to the polls on election day and saw two major party candidates and an independent candidate on the ballot for an office, I would vote for the independent candidate just because I do not like political parties.

I also do not like the news media because they make no secret of their hostility toward independent voters. When independent voters were dismissed in 1988, I went to the office of a major newspaper, talked to a reporter for about an hour, returned home, and received a telephone call from the reporter. He was calling to tell me that his editor was not going to let him write he story. The same situation arose when I sent the article from a local newspaper to major news outlets showing that the two major parties had conspired together to decrease independent voter registration in Arizona. It was a story they refused to cover. Independent voters and independent candidates should expect this kind of treatment from the news media.

Secondly, if the news media does condescend to talk to an independent candidate, they will take one of two attitudes: 1. It is extremely humorous that you would try to run as an independent candidate. 2. You have done something terribly wrong in trying to run for office as an independent candidate. The news media believes that they should be the people who select who candidates for political offices should be. Then they inform the voters the way they should vote on election day. The best way to deal with the news media as an independent voter is to expect nothing good from them. We independent voters believe in freedom of the press. If the news media wants to become irrelevant, they should be allowed to become irrelevant.

Finally, we have no argument with political parties. We just do not like their form of government because they take away our inalienable rights. As independent voters, what we need to do is to use what remains of our individual rights to participate in United

States government. If political parties do not like it, they will continue to do what they have always done. What is there to argue about?

It seems to me that political parties are in a perfect position to show everyone how good political party government can be. They control elections. They control the news media. They control all public offices. They control the people. So, what is the matter political parties?

Could it be that President George Washington was right when he said that political parties were incapable of providing good government in popular governments, in governments purely elective?

The Nazi Party did not provide Germany with good government. The Communist Party did not provide Russia with good government. The Fascist Party did not provide Italy with good government. The claim of American and British parties is that if there are two parties, then it is good government. So each party tries to eliminate the other party. The only thing that the two parties in a two-party system seem to agree on is that independent voters cannot be allowed to participate in the government. My prediction is that political parties in the United States will continue to decline. I do not see that as a bad thing. Citizens of the United States can register as independent voters. The reason they can do that is because when the United States began, all voters were independent voters. Independent voters all over the United States are seeking ballot access in the courts. The Democratic Party controls the judicial system of the United States at the present time. It is futile to ask the Democratic Party to allow participation of independent voters as candidates for political office. Democrats in the past have allowed independent candidates on the ballot, but they have usually been Democrats, and their purpose was to pacify some segment of voters that felt particularly oppressed by showing them the futility of independent candidacy. As long as political parties are appointing judges, the judges are going to rule against independent voters.

The best thing independent voters can do is to start registering as candidates for office, especially for state and local offices. They should also seek appointment as election officials. In Arizona, independent voters can be election officials, but according to present laws, supervisors of election officials have to be party members. Independent voters need to start registering voters in order to protect their right to be voters and candidates for office. There will not be much to vote for in the near future because of the two major parties, but that can be improved over time by the existence of independent candidates.

What I have predicted is going to happen anyway, so we might as well go ahead and do it. Political parties are too incompetent to keep up with the needs of the people, just as they were with the question of slavery. The difference now is that independent voters can keep the major parties from putting together another Civil War. Here in the United States the people are the government. Any time they are complaining about the government, they are complaining about themselves. If they support political parties, they are supporting bad government. I say register the people to vote and let them decide what kind of government they are going to have.

Political parties have proven their limited ability to attract and register voters. People do not really want to vote for corrupt government. Some nations combat this deficiency by requiring the citizens to register to vote. That does not seem to help much. Most people still do not seem to get excited about corrupt political parties. In the United States, independent voters, having achieved a higher rate of voter registration than political parties for the first time since 1800, are going to increase until they control the government. The goals of independent voters will not be specific party contentions, but free and open elections in which the people decide. Independent voters are now discovering that they do not have the same opportunities in government that political party politicians have secured to themselves. There will be a de-Europeanization of American government at the same time party politicians are trying to enforce European political values. The political philosophy of Europe has always been that the people exist to serve the state. This idea was rejected by the American founders and replaced with the idea that the state exists to serve the people. Political parties have now decided that independent voters should serve political parties and that their rights to vote in elections they pay for and to be candidates for political office do not exist.

CHAPTER SIXTEEN

In the final analysis, independent voters will succeed in American government for the same reasons Americans engaged in a war of revolution against Great Britain in the first place. Political parties are too expensive and too inefficient in government to be sustained in government, just as Americans considered the Tory Party to be too expensive to continue to support before the Revolutionary War. We might compare the success of the two-party system of the United States with Napoleon Bonaparte's invasion of Russia.

There has been little opposition to party control since the election of 1800, when a political party came into power in American politics. In like manner, after a stern warning to Napoleon from Russian Czar Alexander, the Russians were almost completely ineffective against the French army of a half million soldiers until the Battle of Borodino, in which the French lost a substantial number of soldiers in removing the last obstacle to the capture of Moscow.

But it was a hollow victory. Most of the inhabitants of Moscow had abandoned their city, and the departing government had set it on fire. There was nothing there to sustain the French army, and as winter began to set in, Napoleon had no choice but to retreat the way he had come. Of his half million army, only 20,000 lived to escape their invasion of Russia.

The difference between the two-party system in the United States and the Grand Armee is that American political party members will not have to die, but will come out of their defeat better off than they were under party control. Except for the engagement at Borodino, the Russian army did not directly confront the French army and did not have as much effect on its defeat as the starvation, disease, and Russian winter into which the great leader of the French army had led his troops.

Here is why the two major parties are done. They are not only incompetent at running the government, they have borrowed too much money. The United States has been out of debt one time in its history. That was during the Presidency of Andrew Jackson. Jackson beat down the National Bank and got the government out of debt. However, a year into the administration of Martin van Buren, Jackson's successor in the Presidency, the Panic of 1837 put the national economy into a recession similar to the one in 2008. The federal government went into debt again, increasing the money borrowed each administration thereafter to its present level of thirty-one trillion dollars. The national debt is the Russian winter that will bring down the two-party system.

When I was growing up during the fifties and sixties, the national debt was a great concern to party leaders. There were spokespersons in both parties who warned against getting further into debt. But there was an arms race going on. World Communism had to be opposed. Poverty had to be stopped in the United States. Government expenditures could not be brought down overnight.

The amount of debt back then seems insignificant compared to the obstacle it is now. But the problem was the same then as it is now. Political parties of today cannot function without increasing the debt. That means that the government of the United States cannot function without increasing the debt as long as political parties control the government. The mistake back then was not the intent of the American people. They intended to pay the debt. Their mistake was in believing that there was a way to reduce and pay the debt through party politics.

Forget paying the debt through political parties. They are only going to increase the debt. After reaching the astronomical figure of five trillion dollars in the 1990's the Republican administration of George W. Bush increased the debt another five trillion dollars to finance two wars during his eight years in office. All of that money expended did not help the national economy. The nation fell into financial disaster as Bush left office. The rate of borrowing increased even more with the Democratic Party administration of Barack Obama. After the borrowing of the Obama, Trump, and Biden administrations, the national debt has now reached thirty-one trillion dollars.

We need to go a different direction. During the first term of President Bill Clinton, the issue of the national debt came to the forefront of party politics. Republicans in Congress, who had control of the legislature, balked at raising the debt ceiling during the term of a Democratic President. The President responded by announcing that he was shutting down the government. It was during this face-off between the President and members of Congress that, after listening to a speech by the President, I signed my income tax return check, which I had just received, and sent it to President Clinton along with a letter requesting that it be applied toward payment of the national debt.

About a week later the check was returned along with a letter from someone on the White House staff explaining that the President could not accept my donation.

That's odd, I thought. I am sure he would have accepted the money if I had said I was donating it to his re-election campaign. I started sending the check to various members of Congress, explaining what had happened when I sent it to the President and asking how the money could be applied toward payment of the debt. Same result. After several tries, I sent the check to a Representative from Arizona named Sam Coppersmith, who styled himself as a Jacksonian Democrat. He seemed to have some of Jackson's knowledge of government finances because he wrote to inform me that he had forwarded my donation to the Bureau of the Public Debt.

Bureau of the Public Debt?

So I started sending a small donation every year to this worthy cause. Each time I would send a donation, I would get a nice letter in return thanking me for my donation and telling me that during the past year, three million and some odd dollars had been contributed to help pay the debt. I found this to be a great advantage when discussing the national debt with political party members on the internet. I would make a little chart like this:

Changes made to the national debt in the last four years

Republicans and Democrats   -$4,000,000,000,000

Independent voters   +$160.00

I had no idea that political party politicians would take it so personally. After some years of discussing the national debt in this manner, during the administration of Barack Obama a notice appeared on the website of the Bureau of the Public Debt.

The Bureau of the Public Debt no longer accepts donations for payment of the public debt. Any money received for this purpose will be put in a general fund and used as Congress directs.

So I stopped trying to pay the Public Debt. The idea of paying the Public Debt has only existed for two brief periods in American government, once when Andrew Jackson had the debt paid off for a little while, and then another time when I was going to pay it.

CHAPTER SEVENTEEN

Americans of today seem to be increasingly disappointed and dissatisfied with their government. Whether you talk to a Democrat or a Republican, they say the same thing: The government is broken. I would take a different approach and say, The government is not broken. Democrats and Republicans do not know how to run the government. As the strong party in two-party corruption, the Democrats are the party to watch. Back after the economic crisis, Democrats were studying what they believed was becoming popular.

"There's something Americans like even less than communism: Congress.

"According to a recent Gallup poll, Congress' approval rating is sitting at only 13 percent, continuing a historic low point in popularity, some have taken it upon themselves to compare this to the popularity of other subjects.

"One such person is Senator Michael Bennett (D-Colo.) who created a chart to help explain just how low these numbers are. Although Gallup puts Congress' popularity at 13 percent, Bennett uses a recent New York Times/CBS poll which found it to be even lower at 9 percent.

"As previously mentioned, one of the subjects was communism—specifically America becoming Communist. According to a Rassmussen poll performed this year, 11 percent of people polled were OK with the idea of America going Communist.

"If that doesn't cause a surprise, some of the other numbers should help. After the oil spill in the Gulf, BP stood at 16 percent, Nixon held 24 percent during Watergate, and banks, were still hovering at 23 percent as of this year, all according to Gallup polls.

"Clearly, Congress is not very popular right now.

"One last figure that some people like to bring up to help hammer the point home is the popularity of King George during the

Revolutionary War. With an estimated 15 to 20 percent of those in the colonies being loyalists, he fares much better than Congress does today." (Failure of Diplomacy: Recent polls show Communism more popular than Congress, The Daily Reveille, July 2, 2012)

Since Democrats want to talk about Communism, we might want to consider an account of a Communist Party meeting.

"A district Party conference was under way in Moscow Province. It was presided over by a new secretary of the District Party Committee, replacing one recently arrested. At the conclusion of the conference, a tribute to Comrade Stalin was called for. Of course, everyone stood up, (just as everyone had leaped to his feet during the conference at every mention of his name). The small hall echoed with "stormy applause, rising to an ovation". For three minutes, four minutes, five minutes, the "stormy applause, rising to an ovation" continued. But palms were getting sore and raised arms were already aching. And the older people were panting from exhaustion. It was becoming insufferably silly even to those who really adored Stalin. However, who would dare to be the first to stop? The Secretary of the District Party Committee could have done it. He was standing on the platform, and it was he who had called for the ovation. But he was a newcomer. He had taken the place of a man who had been arrested. He was afraid! After all, NKVD men were standing in the hall applauding and watching to see who quit first! And in that obscure, small hall, unknown to the Leader, the applause went on—six, seven, eight minutes! They were done for! Their goose was cooked! They couldn't stop now till they collapsed with heart attacks! At the rear of the hall, which was crowded, they could of course cheat a bit, clap less frequently, less vigorously, not so eagerly—but up there with the presidium where everyone could see them? The director of the local paper factory, an independent and strong minded man, stood with the presidium. Aware of all the falsity and all of the impossibility of the situation, he still kept applauding! Nine minutes! Ten! In anguish he watched the secretary of the District Party Committee, but the latter dared not stop. Insanity! To the last man! With make-believe enthusiasm on their faces, looking at each other with faint hope, the district leaders were just going to keep applauding till they fell where they stood, till they were carried out of the hall on stretchers! And even then those who were left would not falter......Then after eleven minutes, the director of the paper factory assumed a businesslike expression and sat down in his seat. And, oh, a miracle took place! Where had the universal, uninhibited, indescribable enthusiasm gone? To a man, everyone else stopped dead and sat down. They had been saved.......That night the factory director was arrested. (The Gulag Archepelago, Aleksander I. Solzhenitsyn, p. 69-70)

There are some government meetings more painful than sessions of Congress. I have to assume that most of the people who responded to the poll about Communism had never read Solzhenitzyn's book. One thing about the spirit of party, it gets everyone doing the same thing.

But the unpopularity of Congress is significant because the legislative branch of government is the branch which represents the people and is the one over which they have the most control. If their own branch of government is the most unpopular with the people, then something obviously is not right, and if Congress is not broken, as both major parties are saying, then it is certainly impaired and in need of attention.

As everyone studied in junior high school, there are three branches of government in the United States, the executive, headed by the President, the legislative, consisting of the two houses of Congress, and the judicial, consisting of the courts and presided over by the Supreme Court. Each state has a similar division of power presided over by a governor at state level. The Vice-President functions in two branches of government, working with the President in the executive branch and presiding over the Senate in the legislative branch. This form of government was patterned after the English government, the major difference being that instead of having a king as head of government, there would be an elected President.

We have already explained what happened to the powers of Congress in the election of 1800. The United States Supreme Court said that it was "striking down" an act of Congress. This totally changed the government of the United States, making Congress the weakest branch of government, with the Supreme Court and the judicial branch as the strongest. George Washington, in his Farewell Address, warned that the three branches of government needed to stay out of the duties and responsibilities of the other branches of government. Having elevated the judicial branch to the position of a Supreme Legislature, political parties seem to interpret the duty of Congress to be to hold endless committee hearings to investigate the actions of members of the political party out of power. The Presidency is also weakened tremendously. The executive branch, including the military and intelligence agencies, take upon themselves the responsibility that kings in Europe once functioned to accomplish. They search the world looking for wars in which young Americans can participate as undeclared combatants.

CHAPTER EIGHTEEN

The principle of government that made American government different from European governments was the idea that federal and state governments were there to serve the needs of the people. In other words, as Thomas Jefferson had written in the Declaration of independence, individual people in the population of a nation had inalienable rights, including, but not limited to, life, liberty, and the pursuit of happiness. When William and Mary deposed King James II in England, Parliament presented to them a Declaration of Rights that the new king and queen were required to agree to uphold before Parliament would confirm their sovereignty. As we have already mentioned, the Declaration of Rights contained two provisions regarding judicial powers that prohibited the "striking down" of acts of Parliament by English courts that had plagued England during the reigns of the Stuart kings and prohibiting the monarchy from acting as judges.

Obviously, the Declaration of Rights was the historical precedent for the American Bill of Rights that some states held out to get adopted at the Constitutional Convention before agreeing to ratify the Constitution. The first ten amendments were the Bill of Rights. There were some amendments dealing with the rights of defendants before American courts, just as there had been similar provisions in the Declaration of Rights, but nothing in the Bill of Rights prohibiting the courts from "striking down" acts of Congress. The neglect of the founders in not being more specific in addressing this separation of powers that was so beneficial to English government and so detrimental to American freedom when the Supreme Court said that it was "striking down" an act of Congress is something that the American people need to address today. "Striking down" an act of Congress enabled the Democratic Party to enforce slavery in the United States for the next sixty years, something that would not have happened if the people of the United States had not supported political parties and the Supreme Court had not proclaimed itself to be more powerful with regard to legislation than Congress.

Neither should Congress interfere with decisions of courts. Courts have every right to say that a law passed by a legislature violates the individual rights of a person before the court, which is what they should have done with regard to slavery. If individual slaves could have gone before United States courts and received justice instead of enforcement of unjust state laws, the issue of slavery could not have endured for sixty more years. You will notice the same disregard for individual rights in modern American politics as politicians talk about "rule of law". The Preamble to the Constitution says there will be liberty and justice for all. Slaves who labored under rule of slavery laws were not receiving liberty or justice. A political party had determined that they were going to be slaves, and the weak opposing party never really did more than compromise concerning slavery.

Today other individual rights are being denied and compromised in the same manner as occurred with the enforcement of slavery because it is beneficial to the power of political parties to deny those rights. Specifically, we can give the example of denial of rights of independent voters to vote in elections they are forced to pay for and denial of the right to be candidates for public office through enforcement of unConstitutional state election laws that exist solely for the purpose of keeping independent candidates off from the ballot. But there are other rights that have disappeared that affect all Americans, including political party members. Foremost among these is the right to trial by jury. The Constitution sets forth the right to trial by jury in all criminal prosecutions in Amendment VI and the right to trial by jury in all civil disputes where the value in controversy shall exceed twenty dollars in Amendment VII. From the beginning Americans were being denied trial by jury, often by mobs who executed people without a trial. But in recent years all states have systematically denied this right. The last state still granting trial by jury in all criminal prosecutions was Montana, which abandoned the practice in the 1990's.

The Constitution also leaves no doubt about whether the Constitution needs to be followed by judges. Article IV(2) This

Constitution, and the laws of the United States which shall be made in pursuance thereof, and all treaties made under the authority of the United States shall be the supreme law of the land, and the judges in every State shall be bound thereby, anything in the Constitution or laws of any State to the contrary notwithstanding.

In other words, judges have no power to amend the Constitution. Article V gives Congress and the states power to amend the Constitution.

Lawyers and judges pay little attention to what the Constitution says, or they would never have embarked on a legislative agenda using the judicial branch of government to "strike down" acts of Congress. The Constitution is also plain about which branch of government regulates the other branch. Article V Section 2(2) The Supreme Court shall have appellate jurisdiction, both as to law and fact, with such exceptions and under such regulations as the Congress shall make.

What should happen in government to correct the situation and to restore Congress to its full authority?

First, it could be done if the President issued an Executive Order directing that it happen, This is what took place when Abraham Lincoln freed slaves with the Emancipation Proclamation. The Supreme Court had declared slavery legal in the United States with the Dred Scott decision in 1856, Lincoln overturned that decision with the Emancipation Proclamation, showing that the executive branch presides over the judicial branch. In terms of what makes the Emancipation Proclamation the law over the Dred Scott decision, the President has the power to grant pardons. If any court in the United States had sentenced anyone to slavery, the President had the power to pardon the person from that unjust court decision.

Second, Congress could regulate the Supreme Court as the Constitution said they had the power to do. If Congress had done its duty in 1803, they would have told the Supreme Court, The Constitution does not give any court authority to "strike down" acts of Congress.

Ideally, an amendment to the Constitution should be made that specifies that courts cannot "strike down" acts of Congress. If a court says that a law is unjust, that can be a proper function of courts, and a ruling can be made however the court deems just in the individual case before the court, but courts should not be empowered to act as legislatures. An extreme example of what can happen when courts claimed to be making laws is what happened in Germany when courts began to sentence to death mentally disabled people, resulting eventually in concentration camps to exterminate Jews. Or we can consider what happened in peoples' courts in the Soviet Union under Josef Stalin, when 12,000,000 Russians were sentenced to death by those courts. The problem that arises is that when one court executes a person unjustly, if decisions of courts are thought of as laws, rather than court opinions, these court decisions can be applied through multiple courts to multiple people, resulting in mass exterminations of people.

Third, the Supreme Court could regulate itself and voluntarily stop "striking down" acts of Congress.

None of these remedies are likely to happen under political parties, but the possibility that they could happen does exist. What Americans should do is expect the worst from political parties and re-declare independence. They do not need to fight a War of Revolution like they did in 1776 or a Civil War like they did in 1860. It has nothing to do with war. All they need to do is register as independent voters.

Political parties may seem to have an insurmountable advantage in American government but it is all based on what George Washington called "artificial authority". Democrats and Republicans give us government of the parties, by the parties, and for the parties. The problem they have is their incompetence in government, resulting in a spontaneous increase in independent voters, causing them to expand from a single digit percentage when John F. Kennedy was President to 49% of registered voters today, according to the latest poll. The only reaction to this increase in independent voters by Democrats and Republicans has been to pass election laws at state level to make it impossible for an independent candidate to appear on the ballot. We can say that these two contentious major parties have one area of bi-partisan agreement left between them as we watch them vote in Congress on straight party lines with regard to bills proposed by legislators from one party or the other. They still agree that independent voters have no place in American government and shall not be allowed to participate except as slaves to two-party control.

Americans should all register as independent voters. The fact that there are people who support political parties does not mean that political parties are good. It means that people feel safer if they belong to an organization which makes all important decisions for them. Independent voters are not an organization and should not try to become anything other than United States citizens registered to vote. They do not need to riot, destroy property, or attempt to force others to their beliefs. They should just vote and be candidates for public office. If there are still more people who want to be in political parties than people who want to be independent, then independent voters should still just vote and be candidates for public office. There is really nothing to argue about. George Washington has been proven correct in his assessment of political parties. Americans should re-declare independence by registering as independent voters.

www.ingramcontent.com/pod-product-compliance
Lightning Source LLC
LaVergne TN
LVHW010559070526
838199LV00063BA/5018